I

Gypsies in the Ottoman Empire

The Interface Collection, coordinated and developed by the Gypsy Research Centre at the Université René Descartes, Paris, is published with the support of the European Commission.

Some Collection titles receive Council of Europe support for distribution in Central and Eastern Europe.

The views expressed in this work are the author's, and do not necessarily reflect those of the publisher nor of the Gypsy Research Centre or its research groups (historians, linguists, education specialists and so on).

Director of the Interface Collection: Jean-Pierre Liégeois
Editorial Co-ordinator: Astrid Thorn Hillig

Cover: Catherine Liégeois
DTP: Frédérique Vilain, GD-Infographie

© 2001
Centre de recherches tsiganes (Gypsy Research Centre) and
University of Hertfordshire Press

University of Hertfordshire
College Lane
Hatfield
Hertfordshire AL10 9AB
UK
Tel. +44 1707 284654
Fax. +44 1707 284666
Internet: UHPress@herts.ac.uk
Web address: http://www.herts.ac.uk/UHPress

ISBN: 1 902806 02 6
Printed in Great-Britain by J.W. Arrowsmith Ltd., Bristol
Published: 2001

Elena Marushiakova
Vesselin Popov

Gypsies in the Ottoman Empire

A contribution to the history of the Balkans

Translated by Olga Apostolova
Edited by Donald Kenrick

Centre de recherches tsiganes
University of Hertfordshire Press

Elena Marushiakova obtained her doctorate at Bratislava University after graduating in Sofia. She is currently working at the Ethnographic Institute and Museum of the Bulgarian Academy of Science.

Vesselin Popov obtained his first degree at Sofia University and his doctorate at the Bulgarian Academy of Sciences. He is currently working at the Ethnographic Institute and Museum of the Bulgarian Academy of Science.

Elena Marushiakova and Vesselin Popov are joint authors of the standard work on the Gypsies of Bulgaria and editors of the collection of books about Roma folklore, *Studii Romani*.

Contents

The Balkans – the second home of the Gypsies 7

The beginning of the Gypsy migrations
    The first stage of migration 12
    The arrival of the Gypsies in the Balkans 13
    The Gypsies in the Byzantine Empire 15
    The Gypsies in the Balkan states 18
    The Gypsies on the eve of the Ottoman invasion 20

The rise and glory of the Ottoman Empire
    The Ottoman invasion of the Balkans 23
    Ottoman conquests and the building of the Empire 24
    Historical sources about the Gypsies in the Empire 26
    The Gypsies in the tax registers 27
    What we learn from the tax registers 28
    The Gypsies – Christians and Muslims 29
    What were the names of the Gypsies? 30
    Law concerning the Gypsies in the province of Rumelia 32
    The Gypsy sanjak – Gypsies in the Ottoman army 34
    The nomadic Gypsies 35
    Settling the Gypsies 38
    Sub-contracting the collection of taxes 39
    How Gypsies earned their living 41
    Conflicts with the law 44
    Loose women 45
    European travellers 46
    Civil status of the Gypsies 46
    Official legislation and everyday reality 47
    Gypsy migrations within the Balkans 50

The decline and twilight of the Ottoman Empire
    The crisis in the Empire and its prolonged agony 51
    Historical sources about the Gypsies 53
    The evidence of Johan Kempelen 55
    Demographic data 55
    The Gypsies and the time of reform 57
    Mustafa Shibil 59
    The nomadic Gypsies 63
    The Gypsy farmworkers 64
    The Gypsy musicians 65
    Gypsy crafts 67

A Gypsy proletariat 69
The national revival of the Balkan people 69
The Gypsy poll-tax in Serbia 70
The Gypsies and the religious institutions 72
Attitudes towards the Gypsies 74
The beginning of Gypsy emancipation 76
The first Romani poet? 79
The slavery of the Gypsies in Wallachia and Moldavia 84
The Gypsy migrations 86

The end of the Ottoman Empire 89

The horror of Kosovo: the legacy of the Ottomans 91

Glossary 93

Notes 97

Bibliography 101

List of illustrations 107

The Balkans – the second home of the Gypsies

Experts on Gypsies often say that the Balkans are 'the second home of the Gypsies' and describe and classify Romani (the language of the Gypsies) as a 'Balkanised Indian language'. This emphasis on the important role that the Balkans played in shaping the history, culture and language of the Gypsy people is not merely a conventional expression, but is based on serious scientific research.

During their journey from distant India to central and western Europe the Romany Gypsies settled in the Balkan peninsula for many centuries. As will be discussed later, there are different theories for the time of their arrival in the Balkans, varying from the ninth to the eleventh centuries, but since they only began to enter western Europe during the fifteenth century they must have lived in the Balkans for at least five. This has had a significant effect on the development of the main characteristics of the Gypsies as a community and on their culture, including their language.

In addition, large numbers of the Gypsy people have remained in the Balkans, living in the territory of the Ottoman Empire and its vassal states (especially the Danube principalities of Moldavia and Wallachia), and subsequently in the states established within the former boundaries of the Ottoman Empire – states which remained linked with it. In modern times significant numbers migrated throughout the world, including the so-called 'Great Invasion of the Kalderari' (or Coppersmiths) during the nineteenth and the twentieth centuries, the waves of migration from former Yugoslavia from the 1960s until the 1980s, the migration from Romania following the changes in eastern Europe in 1989 and that of refugees from Bosnia and Kosovo. They carried with them distinct traces of the cultural and linguistic interaction with other peoples which took place in the historical conditions reigning in the Balkan region.

It is impossible to explain or make sense of the character of the Balkan region without taking into account the role of the Ottoman Empire. For over five centuries it dominated the Balkans and had a profound influence on the overall cultural and historical development of the region, including the states established in the nineteenth and the twentieth centuries – states whose national ideologies were based on opposition to the Empire, on leaving its political framework and trying – not always successfully – to break with its cultural traditions.

This book will concentrate on the Gypsies living in the Balkans since, as will be shown later, a high proportion of the Gypsy population of the Ottoman Empire was concentrated in the Balkans, and therefore there is considerable historical evidence concerning the Gypsies in this region. Moreover, the Ottoman provinces in the Middle East and northern Africa had a different administrative status and, therefore, a different social and political structure which resulted in conditions for the Gypsies being very different from those of the Balkans. Last but not least, one must remember that, unlike the Balkans, the relatively small number of industrial nomads in these other provinces were not Romany. For all these reasons we have decided in the present study to place the emphasis on the Gypsies living in the Balkan territory of the Ottoman Empire.

The book concentrates on presenting the source material rather than on our personal interpretations and aims as far as possible to present a true picture of the life of the Gypsies in the region during this period. The many previous attempts by others to tackle the topic, as well as some general publications on the Gypsies, led us to believe that author interpretations often distort the truth (especially when this has not been properly studied or understood). The Gypsies in the Balkans were not isolated from the overall cultural and historical environment; on the contrary, they were an integral part of it and consequently were greatly influenced by the cultures of the various Balkan peoples. The Ottoman Empire was a key factor in the development of the Gypsy people and studying and understanding this is the primary aim of the present publication.

* * *

An introduction to the history of the Gypsies in the Ottoman Empire presents some serious but unavoidable problems in explaining a social, historical and cultural reality which is largely unfamiliar to the European reader. However, a detailed explanation of all Ottoman terms relating to the administration, the social system, the religious institutions, tax obligations and army ranks as it developed over five centuries would mean writing a new book on the Ottoman Empire, and there is no shortage of such books already. We opted for the use of much of the original Ottoman terminology with the words being transcribed in English. Where possible, short explanations have been given in the text, while in the remaining cases it is hoped that meanings will become clear to the reader from the context in which the terms are used. Those who are interested in the precise meanings of terms can consult the glossary and specialised historical literature on the Ottoman Empire; the bibliography at the end of the book contains some of the most comprehensive books on the topic.

Our colleague and friend Donald Kenrick has contributed greatly to the creation of this book. From the very beginning he helped us with questions, comments and critical notes, supplied us with scientific literature which was impossible to find in Bulgaria and edited the English translation. We would like to express our most sincere gratitude for all his help.

Our gratitude also goes to the translator of this book, Olga Apostolova, who put a great deal of effort into making it accessible to English speaking readers, and to Astrid Thorn Hillig of the Centre de recherches tsiganes in Paris for the care she took in selecting suitable illustrations for the book.

***

Foreign words are put in italics the first time they occur. If they are not explained in the text, or if they occur again, they will be found in the Glossary. Place names which are asterisked have modern names which are listed at the end of the Glossary.

The world map of Edrisi, 1160 A.D.

The beginning of the Gypsy migrations

Scholarship is still faced with a number of unresolved questions concerning the origin of the Romany Gypsies, the reasons their ancestors left India, the date of their departure and the early stages of their migration towards Europe.

Estimates for the beginning of migrations from India and the dispersion of the Gypsies throughout the world vary widely – ranging from the fifth to the fifteenth century. Grounds for the early date are mainly based on the well-known evidence of the Arab historian from the ninth century, Hamza of Isfahan, and of the Persian poet Firdausi in his *Book of the Kings* of 1011. Both authors relate different versions of the story of the Persian Shah Bahram-Gur (420-38). In the story an 'Indian king' is said to have sent the Shah a large group of musicians (Zotti or Luri) and their families, the majority of whom at a later date would have left the country and wandered around the world. According to several authors the events described, although told in a semi-legendary fashion and in much later times, are rooted in historical fact and can be taken to refer to one of the initial stages of Gypsy migration.

The problem of determining the beginning of the migrations is directly connected to attempts to establish through links to historical events the reasons for these movements. There are different theories but the predominant belief is that this was not a single occurrence but a process that lasted for centuries; a process in which the ancestors of the Gypsies (from different *jati*, or castes, and from different regions – mainly of north-west India) for various reasons left their homelands in small groups in order to take the long road to Europe.

It is often thought that the process of migration was given its impetus by the invasions of the White – Ephtalite – Huns from central Asia during the fifth and the sixth centuries and the serious crisis these invasions brought to Indian society including the fall of the Gupta dynasty and the disintegration of the Empire, as well as to the decay of towns, decline of agriculture, famine and the outbreak of epidemics. The Arab invasion of India in the seventh-eighth centuries (especially in the region of Sind) was also a time of deep social and economic crisis that resulted in massive migrations. Later foreign invasions which some authors suggest also gave impetus to migrations by the ancestors of the Gypsies – for example, those of Mahmud Ghaznavi (eleventh century), Mohammed Ghur (twelfth century), even Tamerlane (beginning of the fifteenth century) – are much too late since by then the Gypsies already appear in historical records in Byzantium and Europe. In spite of this one can accept that there was some later Gypsy emigration from India, an assumption which does not contradict the history of the region; for example, during the seventeenth and eighteenth centuries the so-called Hissarsky Pariah, a community which is at present identified as a Gypsy-like group, settled in central Asia.

The first stage of migration

It is impossible to create a precise chronology of these migrations or a detailed reconstruction of the routes that the Gypsies took during their departure from India. Scholars mainly rely on the results of linguistic studies – the development of the Gypsy language, influences of the foreign cultural and economic environment as reflected in certain loan-words and changes in the language – but these can only determine the main routes and stages of migration.

Most linguists agree that the formation of the Gypsy language began in the sixth or the seventh century, while from the eighth-ninth centuries onwards it developed as a separate language under the influence of the majority languages spoken in the area (Persian, Armenian, Greek). Wandering for several centuries throughout the lands of what are today Pakistan, Afghanistan and Iran, and to the south of the Caspian sea, the Gypsies (and their language) divided into two separate branches (speaking the so-called 'ben' and 'phen' dialects respectively, classed by their word for 'sister'). This marks an important stage in the development of the Gypsy language and the Gypsy community as a whole. On reaching northern Mesopotamia and the eastern boundary of the Byzantine Empire towards the end of the tenth and the beginning of the eleventh centuries, the Gypsies split into three major migration groups – the ben-speaking Dom (who took the southern route or stayed in the Middle East), and two phen-speaking groups – the Lom (who took the northern route) and Rom (who took the western route).

The first group of Gypsies headed south-west and gradually settled in Syria and Palestine, from where some continued into Egypt and northern Africa. It is also conceivable that, during the time of the Arab domination of the Iberian peninsula, Gypsies from this group reached the area by the so-called North African route, thus merging with other Gypsy groups arriving in Spain from the north, although most of the authors argue convincingly against this route of Gypsy migration.

The second group of Gypsies headed north and settled in the lands south of the Caucasus (mainly in present-day Armenia and Georgia). According to some hypotheses, members of this group moved even further, along the so-called northern route (through the Caucasus mountains and the northern shores of the Black Sea), and reached the lands of present-day Romania, the Balkans, central and western Europe but most authors doubt this because of the lack of convincing historical and linguistic evidence.

The third and largest group of Gypsy migrants (the phen-speaking Rom) headed west, towards Asia Minor and the Balkans, and from there in due course to central and western Europe. For several centuries these Gypsies were settled permanently within the boundaries of the Byzantine Empire which, at the time, encompassed large areas of Asia Minor and the Balkans.

The arrival of the Gypsies in the Balkans

The earliest reliable evidence concerning the presence of Gypsies in the Balkans dates from the time of the Byzantine Empire, and more precisely to the ninth, tenth and eleventh centuries. Until recently, most experts on Gypsies accepted the theory of the well-known linguist Franz Miklosich that the first definite mention of Gypsies in Byzantium is in the *Life of St George of Athos*, a saint who died in 1065. The *Life*, written around 1100, relates that in 1054, during the reign of Emperor Constantine IX Monomachos, many 'Atsingani' arrived in Constantinople from Samaria. They had no permanent jobs, wandered around the city and were known for their clairvoyant as well as magic skills. During this time many wild beasts penetrated the emperor's gardens, and so the emperor asked the Atsingani to rid him of the beasts. The Atsingani gave the beasts some poisoned meat and they died. Impressed by their magic, the emperor invited them into the palace and asked them to repeat their magic on his dog. However, St George of Athos, who was present, made the sign of the cross over the poisoned meat and the dog was saved, while the Atsingani were expelled from the palace.

Nowadays the majority of experts on Gypsies tend to accept that the name 'Tsigani' or similar sounding names (used mainly for the Gypsies in eastern Europe) are derived from Atsingani or Atsinkani (both names being mentioned in the sources from the period). There are other, often controversial, theories about the origin of the name – for example, from Asinkar (meaning 'blacksmith' in one of the Persian dialects), a term used during the tenth century in Byzantium; from the name of a mythic river in India, the home of the Gypsies; from the name of the travelling Cengari or Cingari (musicians, dancers) in India; or directly from the medieval Greek *Atsinganoi*, meaning 'untouchable'.

However, the real problem lies elsewhere – what does the word Atsingani (or Atsinkani) mean? This question cannot yet be given a definitive answer, due to the fragmentary and ambiguous nature of the historical sources from this period. It used to be thought that this name referred to a Manichean or a similar heretical group involved in various kinds of clairvoyance, palm reading, exorcism and ventriloquism, and that consequently it was transferred (by analogy with their similar practices) to the ancestors of the Gypsies.

Contemporary Byzantium scholars (for example, Paul Speck) believe that the term Atsingani was always used in Byzantine sources to refer to the Gypsies. This new interpretation of the source material places the date of the penetration of the Gypsies into the Byzantine Empire in a much earlier period and is supported by a number of modern linguists.

In Byzantium Atsingani are mentioned in the town of Amorion in the Phrygia region in the *Chronography* by Theophanes the Confessor written around 800. In it we also find a detailed account of the 'fervent friendship' between the Byzantine emperor, Nikephoros I Genik (802-11), and 'the Manichees, now called Pavlikiani', as well as the 'Atsingani living in Phrygia and Likaonia' (i.e. the two groups Pavlikiani and Atsingani are seen as different). The latter had helped the emperor with their knowledge of magic by putting down a riot in 803. For this the emperor permitted them to move freely throughout the Empire, some of them choosing to settle down in Thrace.

Most historians believe they settled in and around the town of Philippopolis (modern Plovdiv) on the Thracian plain. Since the first half of the twentieth century some Bulgarian authors (for example Naiden Sheitanov) connected the settlement of the Atsingani in Thrace between 803-904 with the arrival of the Gypsies but such an early date for their arrival was not seriously considered by most scholars until quite recently.

Gypsies in Bulgaria generally accept this early date and view it in the context of other events from Bulgarian history. For example, there is a legend which, although dating from more recent times, is well known among Gypsies in Bulgaria. According to this legend the Gypsies were the blacksmiths to whom the Bulgarian Khan Krum entrusted the coating in silver of the skull of Emperor Nikephoros I Genik, killed in 811 in the battle of the Vurbishki Pass. According to patriotic Bulgarian legend, the skull was turned into a cup with which the khan then toasted his soldiers.

The second oldest piece of evidence concerning the Atsingani comes from the biography of Saint Atanasia from the island of Egina who lived in the ninth century. In her *Life* there is a description of how during a period of famine she gave away food to 'foreigners called Atsingani'.

The attitude of the Byzantine emperors towards the Atsingani in this period was not consistent. According to Theophanes the Confessor, the emperor

Michael I Rangave (811-3) for a short period of time imposed the death penalty on the heretical 'Manichees, who are now known as Pavlikiani, and the Atsingani from Phrygia and Likaonia' but with the ascension to the throne of the emperor Michael II (820-30), the situation changed. According to detailed information provided by Theophanes Continuatus, Michael II himself came from Amorion in Phrygia, where there were 'many Jews and... Atsingani' and adhered to their heresy which he had 'inherited from his ancestors'. This heresy was a mixture of the beliefs of the two communities. According to Theophanes the Atsingani were baptised but in every other respect were like the Jews, except that they were not circumcised. The young Michael was first involved in cattle breeding, and only later became a soldier of fortune. He was then told by an Atsingan that he would become the emperor, for which prophesy the emperor later treated the Atsingani favourably.

According to some sources, albeit of a later date, a second wave of mass migration by Pavlikiani and Atsingani from the Antioch region and their settlement again in the region of Philippopolis, took place in 969 under Emperor John I Tzimiskes and was organised by the Patriarch of Antioch, Theodore Monach. According to Matei Kopitar, a nineteenth century Slavic man of letters, the mention of travelling nomads called 'Sigani' in a letter by Archbishop Theophilact of Ohrid to Emperor Alexios I Komnenos (at end of the eleventh or beginning of the twelfth century) is a reference to Gypsies.

The Gypsies in the Byzantine Empire

From later sources, we can be quite sure that between the twelfth and the fourteenth centuries the name Atsingani referred specifically to the ancestors of the Gypsies. There is a considerable body of evidence to support this although some of the material is contradictory and not always based on sound historical records.

For example, the twelfth century Byzantine church legislator, Theodore Balsamon, mentions Atsingani carrying snakes wound around their bodies and foretelling the future. In addition, a circular letter from the Patriarch of Constantinople, Anastasios I, dating from the first half of the fourteenth century, cautions the faithful regarding the unacceptability to the church of contacts and relationships with various snake charmers, magicians, clairvoyants, bear-trainers and such like, with a special warning against the Atsingani whom the faithful should not admit into their houses because they 'preach about devilish things'. This is confirmed by Joseph Brienius, writing in the middle of the fourteenth century, who noted that people in the Byzantine Empire were associating daily with magicians, clairvoyants, Atsingani and exorcists. The term 'Atsingani' is used as an insult in two Byzantine satirical poems from the fourteenth century.

Documents from western Europe provide further evidence of a Gypsy presence in the Balkans. Writing in 1322, the Franciscan monk, Simeon Simeonis, mentions slaves brought from the Danube lands whom he had seen in Egypt – black as 'Indians' but with tattooed faces. The same author also notes a group he calls the 'descendants of Ham', whom he has met on Crete, living in black tents and caves, never staying in one place for more than thirty days. A document by a German pilgrim from Cologne, travelling to the Holy Sepulchre in 1340, mentions the Mandopoli, whom the author noticed while in Morea (present-day Greece) and who spoke their own language which no one else understood. A similar name – Mandopolini – is found in a description of Peloponnesos, written in 1350 by Ludolfus de Suthaim. In a fourteenth century Bulgarian version of the Life of St Barbarus many 'Egyptians' are mentioned as living along the Albanian coast in the region of Dyrrachium*. It is plausible that all, or at least some, of these references are to Gypsies living in the Balkans.

Two distinctive names – 'Tsigani' and 'Egyptians' – began to be used during the thirteenth and the fourteenth centuries, a clear distinction being made between the two communities. For example, in the records of the Patriarch of Constantinople, Gregorios II Kyprios (1283-9), special taxes are mentioned that have to be collected from 'the so-called Egyptians and Tsigani' as well as the practice of sub-contracting the collection of these taxes. Tax collectors paid a percentage of the amount due in advance and then recovered the whole sum from the taxpayer.

Most sources dating from this period use just one of the two names – Egyptian or Tsigan. For example, the widow Anna living in the vicinity of the monastery of Xiropotamou on Mount Athos, is mentioned in connection with her new husband who is an Egyptian, and Nikolaos the Egyptian is mentioned as living in the lands of the Lavra monastery.

These pieces of evidence are also interesting because they make it clear that from that time onwards Egyptians begin to be included in the category of the villeins (*parici*), the dependent feudal population in Byzantium.

Egyptians are also mentioned in the fifteenth century Byzantine *Nomokanon* which bars from receiving the Eucharist for five years anyone who asks 'Egyptian women' to foretell their future or invites these women into their houses in order to exorcise a sick person or the like. In 1415 there is a mention of Egyptians who have for a long time been settled in Peloponnesos.

The name 'Egyptians' became very common in the fourteenth and the fifteenth centuries and most authors link its origin with a region known as Little Egypt. The majority of scholars see Little Egypt as being part of Peloponnesos, although there are other theories as well – for example, that Little Egypt is modern Izmir in Asia Minor or the area around Antioch (Antalia in modern Turkey). It is possible that legends about the Gypsies being the kings of Little Egypt arose at this time – the same legends that the Gypsies themselves propagated on their arrival in western Europe in the fifteenth century.

In Byzantine sources from the fourteenth century we occasionally find other names, for example, a satirical poem (*The drunkard's philosophy*) mentions certain *katsivelos* – sievemakers – a word still used in modern Greece for Gypsies. We meet the same term in a 1350 decree of the emperor John V Paleologos confirming the ownership of land of a certain nobleman, together with the villeins living on the land, some of whom are said to be *egypto-katsivelos*.

During the fourteenth century in the Venetian territories in Peloponnesos and the Ionian islands, the practice of giving certain tax privileges and the right of internal self-rule to the Gypsy population was established (a practice which was widespread by the time of the Gypsy penetration into western Europe). For example, in 1444 the Venetian authorities in the town of Nauplia* in eastern Peloponnesos re-confirmed the privileges won by the predecessors of 'Johannes Cinganos' who was a captain of the Gypsies (*drungarius acinganorum*). Pilgrims travelling to the Holy Sepulchre mention repeatedly the Gypsies of

Town of Modon with Gypsy settlement.

the town of Modon*, on the western coast of Peloponnesos. The earliest evidence (1384) is from Leonardo di Nikolo Frescobaldi who writes about the *Romiti* living outside the city walls. A century later, in 1483, according to Bernard von Braidenbach there were 300 families living there – poor, 'black as Ethiopians', dwelling in shacks near the city, while other travellers add that they were ironware-makers. There are also documents from the island of Corfu dating from the second half of the fourteenth century. The first of these documents – dating from 1375 and re-confirmed in 1386 and several more times over the following century – describes the company of the Gypsies (*feodum aciganorum*). Founded for a special purpose, it encompassed Gypsies working as blacksmiths, cauldron-makers and farmers who, under its terms, were freed from paying taxes and other obligations, and were responsible only to their baron (the first baron being Aloysius de Citro) who, however, had previously collected from them various payments in money and kind alike.

By separating the two terms Tsigani and Egyptians, used in the records of the period, one can try to distinguish the waves of Gypsy migrations into the Balkans and on to Europe, although in a strictly hypothetical way. There appear to be two main waves of migration. In one, perhaps the earlier of the two, the Tsigani moved from Constantinople in the direction of the lands of Bulgaria, Serbia, Moldavia and Wallachia. The other wave, of the so-called Egyptians, moved through Little Egypt (wherever this is but most likely on Peloponnesos) and arrived considerably later in the Balkans. The descendants of this second wave are perhaps the communities whose names are derived from Egyptians (*Agupti* in Bulgaria, *Egyuptsi* in Macedonia, *Yevgi* in Albania and *Gifti* in Greece). These communities have now lost their own language and are quite separate from the rest of the Gypsies in the Balkans. Only time and the possible discovery of new historical sources (or the re-examination of familiar ones) will show to what extent such a distinction between the migration waves in the Balkans is well founded.

The Gypsies in the Balkan states

There is evidence that Gypsies penetrated other Balkan lands and states during the fourteenth-fifteenth centuries but some of this evidence is rather controversial. According to the chronicle of Nikephoros Gregora, a group of acrobats arrived in Constantinople from Egypt at the beginning of the fourteenth century (during the reign of Emperor Andronikos II) after a lengthy tour of the Near East. They visited the courts of many local governors in Thrace, Macedonia, the lands of Serbia, and later performed for the king of Serbia, Stephan Dechanski, eventually reaching as far as Spain. The Byzantium scholar George Soulis states that these acrobats were Gypsies.

In 1348 Stephan Dushan, king of Serbia, issued a charter which specified the taxes to be paid by the *Cingarie* who worked as farriers and saddlers, and then presented them together with property and villages to the Monastery of the

Archangels Michael and Gabriel in Prizren. Some authors believe that the *Cegari* presented by the Serbian king Milutin to the Hiliandariou monastery on Mount Athos in 1290 were also Gypsies, but most Serbian historians, following the lead of Franz Miklosich, do not accept this as evidence of a Gypsy presence in Serbian lands, interpreting these words differently – as shoemakers.

There is, however, no doubt that Gypsies entered the Balkans during this period and this is confirmed by contemporary evidence. The 1362 town register of Ragusa* mentions two 'Egyptian' brothers, Vlaho and Vitan, who make silver-coated leather straps, some of which have been deposited with a local goldsmith in exchange for a loan. Gypsies (Tsigani) were mentioned in Zagreb for the first time in 1373 and again in 1378, and in Ljubljana in 1387, while in the period 1387-97 several dozen Gypsies were registered in Zagreb, mainly as butchers and traders, and often appeared before the judiciary for unpaid loans. Gypsies (mainly small traders and musicians) are frequently mentioned in documents from the fifteenth century, in particular a document of 1443 mentions the Bosnian 'Radoiko the Tsigan' as being in debt to traders from Ragusa.

According to legends recorded in later times, the son of the Albanian ruler Lek Dukagin was killed by Gypsies in Montenegro in the fourteenth century. But Lek refused to do away with all Gypsies living in his lands in revenge because 'one does not buy two loaves of bread for a small coin, and for blood spilled once, there is no need to spill more than one blood', thus choosing to stick to the tradition of blood revenge (blood for blood, man for man) rather than punishing all Gypsies.

It is impossible to be absolutely sure about the first contacts between Bulgarians and Gypsies, or the time of the Gypsies' earliest penetration into the lands occupied by Bulgarians, or about when Gypsies began to settle permanently in Bulgarian lands. The often quoted Charter of Rila (1387) of Tsar Ivan Shishman, has led to much misunderstanding. The text refers to the area known as 'Agoupovi Kleti' which Bulgarian and international scholars have often linked with the Gypsies (interpreting it as Agyupti Kleti, meaning 'poor Gypsies'), although the text does not suggest this, since it is clear that all it refers to are seasonal dwellings for herdsmen in the mountains.

Despite the lack of evidence, it can be confidently asserted that the mass settlement of Gypsies in Bulgarian lands took place between the thirteenth and the fourteenth centuries. This allows for some even earlier contact and settlement – for example, the previously mentioned migration of Atsingani to Thrace in the beginning of the ninth century. This confidence is based on the numerous documents recording the presence of Gypsies in Byzantium as well as their advance towards Serbia, Moldavia and Wallachia. Taking into account the geographical position of Bulgaria, the suggestion that Gypsies settled (or at least moved through) Bulgarian lands during this period seems logical. In addition, there is evidence from the fifteenth-sixteenth centuries (see below) that Christian Gypsies considerably outnumbered Muslim Gypsies in the lands of Bulgaria, suggesting that the majority of Gypsies must have settled there prior to the Ottoman invasion and the absorption of Bulgaria into the Ottoman Empire.

From the same period we have the earliest evidence of Gypsies in the principalities of Moldavia and Wallachia, north of the Danube, although their situation there was very different from the rest of the Balkan states. According to a legend, also published in academic literature, the Gypsies were invited by the Moldavian Prince Alexander I, the Good, who in 1417 issued a special charter which guaranteed the Gypsies 'land and air to live, fire and iron to work'. This charter was reported by Michail Kogalniceanu without anyone else having seen the original and the majority of historians (including Romanians) doubt its existence.

What is certain, however, is that the mass penetration of Gypsies into Moldavia and Wallachia was connected with their donation to monasteries as slaves. At that time the practice of donating land and people (villagers, craftsmen or slaves) to the monasteries by local rulers and aristocracy was widespread in the Balkans. For example, in 1340, Serbian nobles donated several Gypsy families to the Holy Virgin monastery in Tismana (in the Carpathians); in 1360 the chieftain Vladislav presented Gypsy families to the monastery of St Anthony in Vodici; in 1385 his nephew Dan I 'ruler and master of all Ungro-Wallachia' presented forty Gypsy families to the monastery of the Holy Virgin in Tismana; in 1387 his heir Jon Mircea confirmed this gift and gave the monastery in Gozia 300 Gypsy families; according to an imperial letter (chrysobull) of 1428, the Prince of Moldavia, Alexander the Good, made a similar gift to the monastery in Bistrita and so on. In this way there gradually evolved an entire legislative system in these two principalities in which the Gypsies (Atsigani) were given a complex slave status, a subject which will be discussed later.

The Gypsies on the eve of the Ottoman invasion

It is evident that there remain many gaps in the early history of Gypsy presence in the Balkans, as well as questions for which there are no conclusive answers, and the solutions proposed are, as yet, no more than hypotheses. It is quite clear, however, that when the Ottoman invasion and conquest of the Balkans started during the fourteenth century there were already Gypsies who had lived in the region for a considerable period. The integration of the Gypsies in the life of the Balkan people took place in various ways – as nomads, travelling actors, settled town craftsmen and traders. In this sense even slavery can be taken as a form of integration. In any case, it is evident that the Gypsies were integrated (although sometimes in unusual ways) into the social and cultural life of the region.

Ottoman army with army musicians before the gates of Buda and Pest.

One should stress that, leaving aside the specific form of slavery existing in Moldavia and Wallachia (and this is unique in the history of the Gypsies), there was no outright hostility towards the Gypsies in the Balkans such as that which became common amongst local communities in western Europe in later times. The sources, although fragmentary, reveal a contemptuous and negative attitude towards the Gypsies but this was not transformed into their systematic persecution by the civic and religious authorities. This is not without analogies elsewhere but is easily explained by the nature of the Byzantine Empire and the Balkan states which were culturally and historically linked to it – the region being a conglomeration of different peoples where the persecution of 'the other' because of ethnicity was the exception rather than the rule.

Musician [A Gypsy?]

The rise and glory of the Ottoman Empire

The Ottoman Empire was among the world's great Empires. It had a major influence on the course of world history as well as on the fate of those peoples who were part of it.

The Ottoman invasion of the Balkans

The reader is reminded that foreign words are put in italics the first time they occur. If they are not explained in the text or if they occur again, they will be found in the Glossary. The modern names of places marked with an asterisk are listed at the end of the Glossary.

The foundation of the Ottoman Empire was the result of the permanent settlement in Asia Minor from the eleventh century onwards of various Turkoman tribes from Central Asia, the last major migration having taken place during the thirteenth century under the pressure of Mongol invasions. At the end of the thirteenth and the beginning of the fourteenth century a Turkoman tribe, led by Emir Ertogrul and his son Othman (1299-1326), succeeded in subjecting the neighbouring kindred tribes and laid the foundations of a new 'Ottoman' Turkic state in Asia Minor which took its name from Othman.

During the reign of the next ruler – Orkhan (1326-59) – the Ottomans took advantage of the internecine wars in the Byzantine Empire and gradually conquered almost the whole of Asia Minor and began their penetration into the Balkans. In 1352 they took the fortress of Tsimpe* on the Gallipoli peninsula and two years later the fortress of Kallipoli. At this time both the Byzantine Empire and the Balkan states were shaken by continual conflicts which led to

The Balkans around 1360.

the foundation of numerous independent and semi-independent small states and feudal possessions. Taking advantage of these circumstances, the Ottoman armies penetrated the Balkans and, during the reign of Sultan Murad (1362-89), gradually took over the whole of Thrace including the towns of Adrianople, Dimotika* and Philippopolis. Adrianople was re-named Edirne by the Turks and turned into the capital of the Ottoman state. The Ottoman invasion spread even further after the battle of Chernomen (Chirmen) where the armies of Vulkashin and Uglesh, independent rulers of parts of Macedonia, were destroyed. In 1382 Sofia fell into the hands of the Ottomans and further possibilities for the expansion of the Ottoman invasion opened up.

Ottoman conquests and the building of the Empire

The fate of the Balkan people was decided at the Battle of Kosovo, when the united armies of several Balkan rulers led by the Serbian King Lazar were defeated, The new sultan, Bayezid I Ildurum (meaning 'Lightning'), went on to conquer both Serbia and the Bulgarian principalities of Turnovo (in 1393) and Vidin (in 1396). His armies crossed the Danube and forced the ruler of Wallachia, Jon Mircea, to become his vassal.

Ottoman Sultans

1.	Othman 1	1299-1324
2.	Orkhan Ghazi	1324-1362
3.	Murad I Hudavendighyar	1362-1389
4.	Bayezid I Ildurum	1389-1402
	Interregnum	1402-1413
5.	Mehmet I Celebi	1413-1421
6.	Murad II Koja	1421-1451
7.	Mehmet II Fatih	1451-1481
8.	Bayezid II Veli	1481-1512
9.	Selim I Yavouz	1512-1520
10.	Suleiman I Kanuni /the Legislator/the Magnificent	1520-1566
11.	Selim II Sarhosh	1566-1574
12.	Murad III	1574-1595
13.	Mehmet III Adli	1595-1603
14.	Ahmet I Bahti	1603-1617
15.	Mustafa I Deli	1617-1618 1622-1623
16.	Othman II Ghench	1618-1622
17.	Murad IV Ghazi	1623-1640
18.	Ibrahim I Deli	1640-1648
19.	Mehmet IV Avjı	1648-1687
20.	Suleiman II	1687-1691
21.	Ahmet II	1691-1695
22.	Mustafa II Ghazi	1695-1703
23.	Ahmet III	1703-1730
24.	Mahmud I Kambur	1730-1754
25.	Othman III	1754-1757
26.	Mustafa III	1757-1774
27.	Abdul-Hamid I	1774-1789
28.	Selim III Jihandar	1789-1807
29.	Mustafa IV	1807-1808
30.	Mahmud II Adli	1808-1839
31.	Abdul Mejid I Ghazi	1839-1861
32.	Abdul-Aziz	1861-1876
33.	Murad V	1876
34.	Abdul Hamid II	1876-1909
35.	Mehmet V Reshat	1909-1918
36.	Mehmet VI Vahideddin	1918-1922
37.	Abdul-Mejid II, Caliph	1922-1924

Gradually, the entire Balkans were conquered by the Ottoman Empire, with Wallachia and Moldavia retaining the special status of vassal principalities. In 1430 Thessaloniki* fell, and in 1453, after a long siege, Sultan Mehmet Fatih (the Conqueror) succeeded in taking Constantinople which was renamed Istanbul and became the new capital of the Empire, replacing Edirne. The conquered lands were included in the territory of the Ottoman Empire which developed its own specific complex military-based adminstrative and economic system that was then applied to the subject population, including the Gypsies.

The Empire expanded its conquests into the Middle East and North Africa as well as into central Europe. It reached its greatest heights in the time of Sultan Suleiman I, the Magnificient (1520-66). Hungary fell after the battle of Mohács in 1526, and further expansion into Europe was halted only by the unsuccessful siege of Vienna in 1539 and the defeat of the Ottoman fleet in the battle of Lepanto in 1571 – a defeat which was brought about by a coalition of Spain and Venice united under the auspices of the Pope.

This was followed by a sequence of less successful Ottoman wars, resulting in a number of military defeats by Austria, Persia, Russia and Venice, leading to the Treaty of Karlowitz, which marked the beginning of the decline of the Empire.

Historical sources about the Gypsies in the Empire

There is considerable historical evidence for a Gypsy presence in the Balkans during the period of Ottoman domination. Although this evidence is often patchy and inconclusive, it does provide an outline of the nature and extent of this presence.

A large number of Gypsies arrived in the Balkans at the time of the Ottoman invasions, either by directly taking part in these invasions (mainly as auxiliary soldiers or as craftsmen serving the army), or by being among the population which accompanied the invasions. Some of these Gypsies went with the army further into Europe, but a considerable number remained in the Balkan lands where they either settled or continued with their nomadic way of life. Along with the existing Gypsy population in the newly conquered territories, these newcomers figure in various official documents dating from this period, mainly in the particularly rich archives of the Ottoman government and local administration (as yet largely unstudied) under the names of Kibts (i.e. Copts), Chingene, Chingane, Chengene, or Chigan (all derived from 'Chin-Machin' – Turkish for China).

These archives include administrative documents, mainly detailed tax registers, and court orders relating to civic, economic, religious and family matters. The Ottoman social, political and economic system was very different from the western European system. At the height of the Ottoman Empire it was a very hierarchical complex interlocking military-based administrative, economic and religious structure under the firm control of the sultan. This complicated system strictly controlled the daily life of the entire population. The inhabitants were also classed hierarchically into various categories, the main two being the true believers (the Muslims) and the subjected Christian population, each one having a different status and varying obligations towards the central state.

One question of methodology which remains unresolved and neglected by most professional historians (though it can creates serious problems) is the extent to which the surviving official documents provide a true picture of the past. This is especially problematic in the case of the Balkans, irrespective of the period and political system being studied. Nevertheless, after taking into account all the possible flaws of the existing historical sources, this rich and so far under-used material provides a starting point for a fresh look at the history of the Gypsies in the time of the Ottoman Empire.

The Gypsies in the tax registers

The nature of the tax registers was determined by the complex military economic system of landed property in the Empire. Nominally the land was the property of the Empire and part of it (the *myulk*) belonged to the sultan personally or to the religious institutions (the *vakuf*). The sultan broke down the imperial land into parts (*timar, ziamet, has*) and divided it amongst the Ottoman military officer class (the *spahis*). He also granted them a share of various taxes in exchange for their undertaking certain military duties – for example, arming and feeding a number of people, and taking part alongside them in military campaigns.

The first mention of Gypsies in the tax documentation of the Ottoman Empire dates from 1430 and is found in the Register of Timars for the Nikopol sanjak or region, in which 431 Gypsy households are registered, 3.5% of the total listed. An important and more comprehensive source, recording the presence of a substantial number of Gypsies in the Ottoman Empire as well as their social standing, is the collection of laws and regulations relating to the population of the province of Rumelia in 1475, the time of Mehmet II Fatih. Rumelia included almost the entire Balkan peninsula, with the exception of regions with various forms of special status (for example, the principalities of Moldavia and Wallachia and Bosnia). From this collection it is clear that all Gypsies at that time, regardless of whether they were Muslim or Christian, paid a poll-tax (otherwise collected only from non-Muslims) of 42 *akche* for the three years covered by the register.

However, another document in this collection tells us that the Muslim Gypsies were prohibited from mixing with Christian Gypsies and would have to pay a higher tax if they did so:

A Muslim Gypsy should not live among infidel Gypsies. He must be among Muslims. However, if he continues to live among infidels, then the poll–tax must be collected from him – the same amount that is collected from the infidels.

The two ordinances are contradictory. The usual practice, however, was for Christians to pay higher taxes than Muslims, as will be shown by the tax registers we cite later in this chapter.

The system according to which the tax was collected from the nomad Gypsies was also specified – the magistrate (*cadi*) must give the power of attorney to a person who would travel with the Gypsies and be responsible for the payment of taxes. In reality the power of attorney was probably given to a representative coming from the Gypsy community itself. Certain categories of Gypsies were exempt from this poll-tax – including those involved in providing services for the army – for example, the Gypsies who lived in fortresses and maintained them, the blacksmiths making or repairing different kinds of arms, the military musicians and other auxiliary troops. The practice of certain tax exemptions for Gypsies in the service of the Empire was kept up until much later, especially in some regions with special status, like Bosnia.

A further, special register has been preserved concerning Christian Gypsies who had to pay the poll-tax. In all probability these Gypsies had settled in the Balkans before the Ottoman conquest. It covers the period from 1487-9 and records Christian Gypsies living in the districts of Istanbul, Viza, Gallipoli, Edirne, Chirmen, Yanboli*, Filibe*, Sofia, Nikopol, Vidin, Kyustendil, Krushevats, Smederevo, Yeni Pazar* and Bosnia – 3,237 households in all plus a further 211 widows' households. According to Ottoman rules, only men who were heads of households, or widows when they had the same status, were classed as taxpayers and paid on behalf of their whole families. Therefore the tax registers recorded only these two categories. The register in question has a special regulation dating from 1491 attached to it which gave the amount of tax due (25 akche annually), and also specified further taxation – a land tax for Christians (*ispenche*) and a charge on the first night of marriage (*kruvnina*)

What we learn from the tax registers

The data from the tax registers gives a clear idea of the demographic development of the Gypsy population in several settlements – for example, the 1489-90 tax register of Filibe recorded 33 households and 5 widows' households; in 1516 the Gypsy households numbered 175; ten years later there were already 283, of which 90 were Muslim and 193 Christian. In 1516 in Plevne* 11 Gypsy households were registered; in 1550 they numbered 36, while in 1579 there were 44 Gypsy households. This data also gives an idea of the relative percentage of Gypsies in comparison with the rest of the population – for example, in 1526-8 in the district of Eski Zaara* of 2,450 households, 61 were Gypsy households; in 1595 in the town of Yanboli of 529 households only seven were Gypsy households.

The next tax register which deserves particular attention dates from 1522-3 and is entitled *Comprehensive roll of the income and taxation of the Gypsies of the province of Rumelia, who are found in the vakufs of the late Sultan Bayezid khan ... in the vakufs and myulks of the grand ministers and noblemen, in the Gypsy sanjak and in the ziamets and timars*. This vast register consisted of 347 pages and dealt specifically with the Gypsies. It recorded the number of Gypsy households classified according to tax communities, situated in nine judicial districts as well as the religious structure of the Gypsy population, the districts where they lived, their occupation and legal status. The register recorded 10,294 Christian and 4,203 Muslim Gypsy households (in the total were included a further 471 widows' households). Apart from the above, there were a further 2,694 Muslim households in the 'Gypsy sanjak'. According to the calculations of the Macedonian historian Alexander Stojanovsky, whose estimate is based on each household having an average of 5 people, after allowing for some adjustments, this made a total of 66,000 Gypsies, of which about 47,000 were Christian. According to further calculations based on this register there were 17,191 Gypsy households in what became the territory of the present-day Balkan states which were distributed as follows: Turkey 3,185, Greece 2, 512, Albania 374, former Yugoslavia 4,382 and Bulgaria 5,701, while the exact locality of 1,037 households is uncertain. This clearly shows that there were more Gypsies in the Bulgarian lands at that time than elsewhere in the Balkans.

The Gypsies – Christians and Muslims

Additional evidence can be deduced from the Rumelia tax register of 1522-3. In spite of the variety of taxes that had to be paid there was no substantial difference between the taxes paid by the Christian Gypsies and the Muslim Gypsies – for example, the Christian heads of households had to pay 25 akche for their land tax, while the Muslims paid 22 akche, the equivalent land tax for Muslims (*resm-i chift*). The remaining financial obligations were either the same or very similar, including various charges (*baduhava, resm-i arush*) and fines for crimes and infractions (*jyuryum-i jinaet*).

An analysis of the first names of Gypsies gives us an opportunity to consider their religious affiliation. Gypsies who were recorded as being Muslim often had Christian-style names (without being recorded as 'son of Abdullah' which was the standard formula for new converts to the Muslim faith) and vice versa – Christian Gypsies had Muslim names.

In the tax community (*jemaat*) headed by Yani in the Punar Hisar district, Mahmud, Yani's brother, Koja Mahmud and Paraskev, the son of Kasim were recorded as Christians; in the community of Turali, the son of Husain from the district of Yanboli, Kostas, the son of Anastas, Tasos, the brother of Nikola, and Nikola, the son of Kuchar, were recorded as Muslims, while Husain Kethuda and his son Turali, Resim, the brother of Tatar, Husain, his brother, Arnavud, the brother of Seidi, Dervish, the brother of

Kuriz (?) and Ibrahim Hruzo were recorded as Christian; in the community of Goros (Guros), the son of Muhos from the district Eski Zaara, Kalin, the son of Ivan, and Bogdan, the brother of Paskal, were listed among the Muslims, while Iskender and Hamza, the brothers of Matosh, Yankos, the son of Ismail, Ivan, the son of Iskender, and Ibrahim, his son, were included among the Christians.

This evidence demonstrates that the system by which Gypsies were named was very mixed, using Christian and Muslim names, which may have also reflected the syncretic character of their beliefs, often changing with circumstances.

There is another interesting and, to a large extent, inexplicable piece of information in this register – almost all the names of Gypsy women are Christian. The Turkish historian, M. T. Gökbilgin, suggests that, because of their nomadic way of life, the Gypsies had preserved a form of matriarchy in family and clan, honouring the eldest woman who was the keeper of Gypsy customs. This explanation is, of course, hypothetical but not unreasonable, and deserves further investigation.

What were the names of the Gypsies?

The Tax Register of 1522-3 is also an important source for the names of Gypsies of taxable age. Some are hard to decipher (indicated in the list below with a question mark) and most were also used by the surrounding population with only a few showing a connection to the Gypsy language (*Romani*). It is uncertain whether this can be attributed to the frequent use of two names by of Gypsies in the Balkans – the official registration of one name for the authorities and the use of their own name within the community.

The list of names is given in alphabetical order but when the name is a composite one (i.e. made up of several individual names), or accompanied by a nickname (either personal or family) or some other clarification, it is listed separately, as in the case of Abdula Vrana, Gyuro Tarlich, Bali Pancho (Baycho), Kara Hamza, Kyor Stepan, Ma[y]stor Yorghi, Elekchi Iusuf, Simarisa hekim, Ali beg, etc. The different phonetic variants of the same name are also written separately (e.g. Balo and Balyo, Goro and Goros, Gyura and Gyuro, etc.). From the list we can see that the most popular names of the Gypsies with different phonetic variants were: Nikola (Kole, Koyo...); Ioan (Yovan, Ivan, Yanko, Yani, Yano, Yankos...); Dimitri (Dimo, Dimko, Dimos...); Mihal (Miho, Mihos...); Todor; Kostadin (with variant Kostas, Kosta...). If a name is mentioned more than once the number of times it occurs in the register is given in brackets after the name.

Abdula Vrana, Abdulah, Aydin, Aydin Bratula, Alagyoz, Aleksiy, Ali [2], Ali beg, Angel [2], Anastas, Andreya [4], Arap, Arnavud, Ahiryan Dimitri, Ahmed, Ayas
Baze, Bayko, Bayo [3], Bayraklu, Baychina, Bayche, Bakan, Balaban [2], Bali beg, Bali Pancho (Baycho), Balyo, Balo, Barakin, Barba, Barko, Barhina, Bastala, Batiya (Tadiya), Bato, Basha, Bashilko, Begiyata (?), Bezhan, Bezarli [4], Behadir, Biksha Shushuy, Bogdan [2], Boge, Bozhich, Boyko, Boro, Bosilko, Brayo, Branila, Branich, Branko [2], Brato, Brasho, Brayan, Bulaki,

Bulash[2], Burhan, Buyuk Siklu Hadzhi

Chavli, Chakar, Chapukli, Chekriya, Cheshnidzhi Bulat (?), Chiyo, Chiko Zerker, Chilingir, Chuho, Chuche, Chuchman

Dabe, Daverli, David, Davud, Damyan, Dano, Darko, Dasa, Devali, Dede, Dedo, Deli Yovan, Deli Yonus, Deli Nikola, Dervish [2], Dervish Ali, Dzhafer Yorgi, Dzhaho, Dzhebeli, Dzhidzhiko, Dzhiro, Dzhura, Dzhuta, Div (Diyo), Dimko, Dimio [2], Dimo [6], Dimo Vlahot, Dimo Petri Mina, Dimos Rayko, Dimitri [8], Dimitri Pilo, Dobre, Dobrin, Dobroslav, Dogan, Draga, Dragi, Dragichko, Dragman, Dragomir Zerker, Dragos, Dushno, Dudesh, Dudo, Duyko, Duka [3]

Evrenos, Egorida, Eidzhe Kasim Dervish, Elez Duka, Elekchi Yusuf, Erino, Efendo, Efendopul, Eflak Kosta

Faka, Filip, Filip Chingar, Filur, Foka Gyuro, Frko

Gayto, Gano, Gaya, Ginche Novak, Giralyalu, Gogo [2], Goro, Goros, Grdlu, Gucheri, Gyura [2], Gyuro [2], Gyuro Tarlich

Hayman, Hakim Bali, Hamza, Hasan [2], Hirgota, Hristo, Hruso [2], Humbo, Husein (2), Husein Kethuda

Ibraim, Ibrahim, Ibrahim Hruzo, Ivan (2), Ivliya, Ivrada, Ivrana, Ivo, Ilias [2], Isa Bali, Iskender (2), Ismail (2), Ismail Nikola, Istoyan [2]

Kaliya [2], Kalin, Kalkan, Kalko, Kalodi, Kalos, Kalun, Kama Machuka, Kara Vasil, Kara Vida, Kara Gyorgo, Kara Dimitri, Kara Yovan, Kara Oglan [4], Kara Hamza, Karagyoz (3), Karagyoz Aydin Iskender, Karagyoz Oglanlar, Karagyoz Tutuyko, Karadzha [4], Karli, Kastaba, Kastoriyan, Kasim, Kasino (?), Kachiki, Kebeshir Mahmud, Kemanchedzhi Hizir, Kilich, Kir Andreya, Kir Karas, Kiriyak, Kiriyaki, Kiriyako, Kitan, Kircho, Klimo, Kodzha Barak, Kodzha Mahmud, Kodzha Hazar, Koili, Koyko, Koyo [3], Koychin, Kole, Komnin, Kosta, Kostadin [3], Kostas, Kosto, Kochpar, Koshta, Kraguy [2], Krayko (?), Krachayko, Kukich, Kulagyoz, Kulak Stepan, Kuma Nikola, Kuman [2], Kuriz (?), Kurt, Kurtak(i), Kuchar, Kucheri, Kuchi, Kushi, Kyose Balaban, Kyose Boye, Kyose Novak, Kyose Paro, Kyor Stepan, Kyuchuk Kasto

Lazar, Lalamos, Lala [2], Lale, Lalko, Lambo, Laskari, Lola (Lula), Luka

Mavzari, Malkoch, Mamalasin, Manasiya [2], Mangina, Mano [2], Manol, Mare, Marko [2], Marko Mustafa, Martin, Marto, Ma[y]stor Yorgi [2], Ma[y]stor Yan [3], Ma[y]stor Mihal, Ma[y]stor Nikola, Mato, Matosh, Mahmud, Meltush Pashta, Meltush P[e]rchiya, Mehmed, Milahrin, Mile, Milko, Mirksha, Mislakan, Mihal [2], Miho [6], Miho Peluna, Mihos, Moto, Muzafer, Muzevir Duka, Muzevir Efendich, Muzik[i], Murad, Musa [3], Muselem Mustafa, Musliman Kara Hamza bin Abdulah, Musliman Pisho, Musliman Khurukhay, Mustafa [3], Mustra, Muhos

Naim Karadzha, Nako, Narandzhi, Naldzhi Kasim, Nasuh, Nesran, Nikola [14], Nikola Keshish, Nine, Novak [2]

Oliver [2], Oruch

Pagoslu, Papandropa (?), Pazo, Paraskev, Paros, Paskal, Pati, Pachan, Peyo [5], Pencho, Petko, Petros, Pechi, Piperko, Pinari Ogullar, Plav, Priezda [2], Prodan, Polistra, Pribo

Rad [3], Radosav, Radoslav, Radul, Rayan, Rayko [4], Rayo, Rale, Ramazan [2], Resim, Ribica, Riyos Musos, Richa, Richalu, Rund (?)

Sakı, Sara Konstandin, Sarko, Seydi, Sefer Kasto, Shamlular, Shizo, Shiyo, Shirmerd [3], Shirmerd Pancho, Shisho, Shumos, Shurko, Sive Deli Belina, Silen, Simarisa hekim, Simko, Simo Zerker, Sinadin, Sinan [2], Sirovin (?), Sokovali (?) beg, Stepan [3], Suleyman, Sufi Mustafa, Suho Garlo

Tazile, Tasos, Tatar [4], Tatas, Tato [2], Tatos [3], Tatochi, Tatosh, Tatoshin [2], Tasho, Teviki, Teto, Tigran, Timerdzhi Hizir, Tomas, Todor [7], Trushanlu, Tsotsolas, Tuin Rayko, Turali (2), Turshanba

Uglash, Uglesh Nonko, Ugrin [2]

Vardar, Vardo, Vasil [2], Vlad, Vladain Yano, Vladak Shushuy, Vlayko [2], Vlaya, Vogos Butash, Voyvoda, Vranka, Valkashin

Zezo (?), Zhupan, Zlatar, Zuraliya,

Yako, Yand, Yani [3], Yani Chakal, Yani Chiruz, Yanko [3], Yankos, Yankula, Yano [3], Yaramaz, Yarcho, Yahshi, Yachko, Yayan Dimo, Yovan [11], Yovcho, Yoga, Yonus [2], Yorgi [2], Yorgi Kaloyer, Yorgi Pandim, Yorgo, Yorgo Ila (?) Puchi, Yoryo (Boryo), Yusuf, Yusuf Ogullar, Yuhino

The names of the Gypsies as given in the tax register for Rumelia (1522-3).

Law concerning the Gypsies in the province of Rumelia

The Law concerning the Gypsies in the province of Rumelia (*Kanunname-i Kibtiyan-i vilayet-i Rumili*) issued by Sultan Suleiman I the Magnificent in 1530 helps us to a better understanding of the information gleaned from the tax registers. The law stipulated:

1. The Muslim Gypsies from Stambul, Edirne and elsewhere in Rumelia pay 22 akche for each household and each unmarried person. The infidel (Christian) Gypsies pay 25 akche, and, as for the widows, they pay one akche tax (*resim*).
2. The wives of the Gypsies from Istanbul, Edirne, Filibe and Sofia, who have undertaken professions which are unlawful, pay a tax of 100 akche in total each month to the judicial authorities.
3. They pay the charge for marriage as well as the fines for crimes and wrongdoings as do the rest of the subject people, according to the requirements of the law.
4. The Gypsies who show obstinacy and stray from their judicial district, hiding in another district as well as in backyards, are to be found, admonished, strictly punished and brought back to their district. The finding and returning of Gypsies who stray from their community is entrusted to the leaders of their companies and to their village mayors, as well as to others who are suited to this work. [This should be done], so that they are present and do not hide their whereabouts when taxes are due to the sultan or special taxes have to be paid.
5. The fines, the usual taxes and penalties for severe criminal offences, together with the *baduhava* tax imposed on the Gypsies from the Gypsy sanjak, belong to the chief of the Gypsy sanjak. No one from the local administration or any military person should interfere.

    An exception to this are the Gypsies who are recorded as villeins in the prebends, fiefdoms, fiefs and the sultan's lands.
6. The taxes on the Gypsies from the above-mentioned feudal lands are collected from the leader of the subject peoples. The chief of the Gypsy sanjak, the chiefs of the regions in each province, the police and others have no right to interfere with them
7. If Muslim Gypsies begin to nomadise with non-Muslim Gypsies, live with them and mix with them, they should be admonished; after being punished, the infidel Gypsies pay their taxes as usual.
8. Those Gypsies who are in possession of an authorisation from the sultan are to pay only the sultan's tax (*harach-i padishahi*) and do not pay land tax ... and the other usual taxes.
9. The Gypsies of the Branichevo district and the Smederevo region pay 80 akche as rates for each household.
10. The chief of the Gypsies from the province of Nikopol (in times of war) serves in the Nikopol region.

11. The Gypsies from the province of Nikopol, who pay land tax for each household, give 6 akche to their assigned representative, as the equivalent of the fees.
12. The chiefs of the Gypsies of Nish (in time of war) serve in the Smederevo region. The rest of the feudal officers usually serve in the Pasha region.

This law once more demonstrates the special position of the Gypsies in relation to the two main groups in the Ottoman Empire, the true believers (the Muslims) and the rayah (the Christians). It confirmed that the Muslim Gypsies (heads of households and unmarried men) paid 22 akche, while the infidel Gypsies paid 25 akche. Moreover, both categories paid the marriage charge and fines for crimes and wrongdoings as did 'the rest of the rayah', i.e. in this respect there was no difference between them. In addition, the discrepancies between the different categories of Gypsies, with the exception of those included in the so-called Gypsy sanjak, were not clearly and coherently outlined. It is not clear from the text whether the so-called "chiefs of the Gypsies" from the province of Nikopol, who had military obligations and were members of Ottoman military administration, were in fact Gypsies.

Decree of Sultan Selim II in 1574.

This law also reveals the ambition of the Ottoman administration to ensure that taxes were collected in full from everyone, including the nomadic Gypsies, to whom special attention was to be paid by the tax authorities. Members of the Gypsy communities were made responsible for the collection of taxes as a guarantee that they would be paid on time and were also made responsible for the non-payment of taxes to the authorities. As a result, we should not be surprised that certain rights of self-government and relative legal independence were guaranteed to the Gypsies by law. This is confirmed by further evidence, for example a decree by Sultan Selim II in 1574, which obliged Gypsy mine workers from Banya Luka, who enjoyed a special status, to form groups of fifty, each group choosing its 'boss' who was then responsible for them to the authorities.

Selim's decree reads:

The Gypsy communities who are found in Bosnia are entirely freed from the personal tax (*m'af*), from the other occasional taxes (*takalif-i yorfiye*), and from any additional taxes (*avariz*). For the above mentioned Gypsies, one of their own should be elected and appointed for each group of 50 to be the leader (*jemaat bashi*). No one should interfere in his affairs, or limit him in any way. If anyone should break the law, they should be detained and, provided that guarantees are given by the community, and by its leader, there should be an oral hearing. It has been decided that they [the Gypsies] should work in the pits near Kamengrad and should be provided with means for their existence. [This also applies to] the group which is situated outside Novi Pazar (Yeni Pazar). Furthermore, I order that when the Sultan's decree arrives, you should look into this problem.

You should carefully check whether the above mentioned Gypsies are capable of working in the pits, on the condition that they are free from tax, as outlined above. You should also seek the advice, as you think it best fitting, from the appropriate people and persons who are trusted by the Sultan. After that you should register and list in the rolls the Gypsies in question, being as precise as possible and send us the details of the situation.

The Gypsy sanjak – Gypsies in the Ottoman army

The law quoted above confirms the special administrative, legal status and extended rights to taxation and self-government of those living in the Gypsy sanjak (*Cingene sancagi or Liva-i Kibtiyan*). There was also a special law for the sanjak, *Law concerning the leader of the Gypsy sanjak* (1541), which mainly repeats in more detail the key points of the law quoted above. In this case 'sanjak' is not used in the usual sense of a territorial unit but in the sense of a group of the Gypsy population comprising auxiliaries in the service of the army. The Gypsies in this sanjak were grouped into platoons (*myusyulems*) while their auxiliary units (*yamaks*) had their bases near Ottoman fortresses. At the head of each company was the major (*mir-liva*), a non-Gypsy, who was in charge of four captains and eleven corporals. The head of this sanjak, the Gypsy sanjak-chief, was based in the town of Kirk Klise (in modern Turkey) and it comprised Gypsy households from Hairabolu, Viza, Keshan, Chorlu, Punar Hisar, Dimotika, Gyumyurjina*, Fere, Eski Zaara, Yanboli and other areas, mainly in what is today Thrace. For their service the companies (numbering 543) received 449 areas of land in seventeen regions of Rumelia. This practice originated in Anatolia but was modified and widely applied to the Gypsies in the Balkans. The members of the companies undertook auxiliary military duties but not active military service.

Gypsies were also recruited into the army. There is evidence from 1566 that some of the members of the taxable population called up for military duties (*ojaks*) were Muslim Gypsies, alongside the large number of recruits from the Turkish cattle-breeders, the *Yuruks*, who came to the Balkans from Asia Minor at this time. Paul Rycaut, calculated that there were between 4,721 and 5,000 such recruits in the Ottoman army during the seventeenth century, of whom 521 were Gypsies. Every year, five in every thirty recruits were enlisted in the regular army, while the other twenty-five were assigned to provide auxiliary services behind the front line. If Rycaut's figures are correct there must have been between 15,000 and 20,000 Gypsies in the Ottoman army during the sixteenth and the seventeenth centuries.

Gypsies continued to be used in the Ottoman army until the end of the eighteenth century. A Serbian monk, sending secret messages to the Austrian army, reported in 1737 that the defence of Kosovo was left in the hands of the Gypsies, while in 1788 the Gypsies again took part in the defence of Kosovo from the Austrian invaders.

The nomadic Gypsies

The penalties for Muslim Gypsies who 'wandered' (i.e. followed a nomadic way of life) alongside non-Muslim Gypsies were contradictory to the basic principles of tax policy in the Ottoman Empire which was for Muslims to pay less tax than Christians or Jews. The reasoning behind this policy becomes clear from the previously quoted Law concerning the Gypsies in the province of Rumelia issued by Suleiman the Magnificent, where it is explained in detail that Gypsies who nomadised outside their judicial districts had to be sought out and returned so that they could fulfil their tax obligations. The problem was not so much the association of the Muslim Gypsies with non-Muslims but the fact that by travelling they did not pay their taxes regularly. A note attached to the above cited 1498 tax register is significant in this respect. It concerns 'Marko Mustafa's company' which consisted of Muslims who had recently converted from Christianity:

It is the sultan who has ordered that Muslims who leave the company must pay the land tax like all infidels.

In some cases tax policy was a way of regulating the movement of Gypsies within the boundaries of the Empire as well as a way of changing the existing demographic structure in certain regions. For example, a sultan's decree from 1637 lists the taxes and fees that the Gypsies had to pay – poll-tax, land tax and many others (*yuva, kachkun, baduhava,* etc). In total the Muslim Gypsies had to pay 650 akche, while the non-Muslims paid 720 akche, the difference between the two being no greater than in earlier years. However, in the new sultan's order of the following year, 1638, the poll-tax for Muslim Gypsies living in the region of Rumelia was fixed at 200 akche, while Muslim Gypsies and similar nomadic groups recently arrived from Anatolia (Asia Minor) did not have to pay this tax. The amount of other taxes and fees that were to be paid by these two groups also varied, a distinction which is not usually encountered elsewhere.

The surviving Ottoman documents from this period reflect in a great detail the desire of the administration to incorporate the Gypsy population in its registers and to make it pay the necessary taxes. The age, occupation and family status of the Gypsies is given and, along with other factors, used to group them into tax units (communities), each with its respective leader; the communities were in turn divided into smaller units based on the Gypsy quarter in each village or town. Each of these had its own leader, known as *kethuda*, or *ser-i jemaat*, thus applying the principle of limited group responsibility which was typical of the Ottoman attitude towards the subject peoples in its Empire.

The documents always linked the tax community with a specific territorial unit, even in the case of nomadic Gypsies, referred to as *gezende* (meaning 'wanderers') but the extent to which the inclusion of the nomads was successful and complete is unclear, since the register of 1522-3 records only eleven nomadic groups registered for tax purposes in certain villages. For example:

Mustafa Pasha's fiefs.

Filibe district:

... The nomads of Pachan, the son of Bayo; they come from Sofia, live in the village of Mirkovo with the local Gypsies under the administration of the leader of the Gypsies: Christian families seven, income 210 akche.

 Lofcha* district:

... Community of the Miho Pelun's nomads; to be found in the marshes of Plevne: Christian families 7, income 217 akche.

A document from 1551 illustrates the Ottoman administration's desire to make the nomads lead a settled way of life:

Groups of Gypsies ride fine horses. They do not stay in the same place but move from town to town, from place to place. They plunder and steal, thus troubling the population and causing unrest. Since there is no regulation whatsoever as to riding, nor a ban on horses suitable for riding, I have instructed that when a Gypsy tribe is presented, standing under the flag on the throne, it must be informed in advance that it may not ride any horses, but use donkeys and oxen instead. In addition they have to renounce their nomadic way of life, to settle down and to take up farming. The Gypsies must from now on be forced to sell their horses, and if anyone objects they must be punished with a prison sentence.

This regulation was repeated in 1574 and was even extended to the Gypsy acrobats in Istanbul who were banned from using horses. However, it is evident that these, and possibly other such administrative measures, like the 1630 decree of Sultan Murad IV which attempted to force the Gypsies into settling down and adopting permanent residences, were unsuccessful. In practice, it was impossible to force all nomadic Gypsies to settle down permanently, nor did the authorities look upon them as a serious problem. There is, however, evidence of other measures to achieve this aim being introduced – for example, special instructions have been preserved describing how to deal with Gypsies who often change their residence (i.e. led a nomadic way of life). A decree issued by the provincial governor of Bosnia in 1799 reads as follows:

In the past, guarantees were given that there would be regulations as to how the Gypsies should settle down in the cities, in order to take up crafts and not travel. In spite of this, we are informed that the group [of Gypsies] already mentioned have left their craftwork in order to travel around the villages and do evil things like theft and arson, and in this foolish manner to cause harm. Therefore, make an order that the above mentioned group, when it is discovered in the act of crime, is caught and punished by the law.

In reality, the nomadic Gypsies were included in the official administration documents only in connection with temporary (usually winter) settlement. The model of seasonal or irregular nomadism – travel during the warm season and spending the winter in one place – was dominant in the Balkans. We do not know whether this pattern of life was one the Gypsies had brought with them or whether it was forced on them by the social and economic circumstances in the Balkans, and what the role of the Ottoman administration was in this respect, bearing in mind their determination to have the Gypsies included in tax registers and linked with particular villages. In any case, most information from this period reflects the life of the nomads while they were stopping in populated areas.

Some idea of the life of the Gypsies when they were travelling can be gained from the evidence of judicial proceedings. For example, there is a complaint preserved from 1634 by villagers from Srptsi Pasha, in the judicial district of Bitola:

... Nomadic Gypsies often come to our village, live in empty houses and barns, and ... steal hens, lambs, sheep, clothes, and cut down trees and woods. They only cause us trouble and we ask for them to be banned from coming to our village ...

The decision of the court was a compromise: 'the nomadic Gypsies may come into the village but must pay for the damage they have caused'. In a similar complaint, also recorded in the judicial proceedings of Bitola but dating from 1636, the villagers of Jabiani in Bitola district complained about the 'homeless and quarrelsome' Gypsies who steal and damage the village fields. In this case, however, the decision of the court was different, categorically banning the Gypsy groups from settling in this, as well as in neighbouring villages.

Settling the Gypsies

Under the Ottoman Empire, an active process of settlement of Gypsies took place in Balkan towns and villages. The Gypsies who settled down lived in isolated Gypsy quarters (mahallas) – a basic principle of settlement for all minority communities in the Ottoman Empire. The settlement process was very extensive but naturally did not encompass all Gypsies living in the territory of the Empire. Alongside this, a new pattern of a semi-nomadic way of life became more and more widespread, with a fixed winter base but large-scale seasonal nomadism within the boundaries of one district. It is not surprising that in the previously mentioned tax register of 1522-3 the majority of the Gypsies (including those listed as nomads) had a place of permanent residence. A similar process of settling down probably took place in Anatolia. At the beginning of the seventeenth century the well known Ottoman traveller Evlia Çelebi (1611-79) remarked that the majority of the Gypsies living there were settled.

In some cases the Gypsies even abandoned their traditional occupations and became involved in agriculture which they practised within the framework of the existing feudal possessions of the military officers. For example, in an inventory of fiefdoms in the Sofia region dating to 1445-6 there is detailed information on one belonging to Ali, the adopted son of Kara Haji, transferred in 1447 to Sat, the son of Ali of Edirne, which included the villages of Orlandovtsi (today a part of Sofia), Rakovitsa (in the Sofia district), Grapa (in the Pirot district) and Dabijiv (still unlocated, probably disappeared). The last (and smallest) village of Dabijiv deserves special attention. It consisted of 15 complete and 3 widows' households, of which the inventory categorically states 'they are Gypsies'. A comparison of the income of the chiefs of the villages shows that while in Orlandovtsi and Grapa the chief received an average of 91 akche from each household, and in Rakovitsa an average of 43 but in Dabijiv he received an average of only 16 akche from each household, meaning that the Gypsies in this fiefdom stood on the lowest rung of the social ladder.

A few decades later the village of Dabijiv is again mentioned in an inventory of the fiefdom belonging to Sat, the son of Ali, in the Sofia and Samokov districts, dating roughly from the third quarter of the fifteenth century. Once more it is confirmed that 'they are Gypsies' but only five households are recorded – those of Kaloyan, the son of Nikola; of Kaloman, the son of Rad; of Koyo, the son of Lesko; of Jure, the son of Raditsa, and of Fudail, the son of Abdullah. It is evident that the number of taxpayers had decreased which was probably due to their move to other feudal lands. The appearance of Muslim Gypsy names can also be noted – the formula 'son of Abdullah' found here was standard and, as mentioned previously, was used to indicate newly converted Muslims.

Some historians (M.T. Gokbilgin in particular) argued on the evidence from the 1522-3 register (in which dues paid to the state in the form of farm produce are almost entirely lacking) that the involvement of the Gypsies in agricultural work was merely sporadic and in the majority of cases the Gypsies continued to maintain certain professions and crafts. However, most authors are inclined to believe that in this case an explanation must be sought in the special status of the Gypsies and the overall specific character of the Ottoman tax system which was linked to land use. To confirm this, we can cite an example of the existing practice described in the Law of the Silistra region dating from 1569, where a Gypsy tax community is mentioned, in which there are twelve households and seven unmarried taxpayers whose obligations are as follows:

... The Gypsies who stop in fiefdoms and occupy land, pay the tithe and the charges relating to the land, to the owner of the land, while they must pay the rest of their taxes in the district where they paid them before.

Information contained in the judicial proceedings of the Sofia region from the beginning of the seventeenth century listed among the taxes paid by the Gypsies a one-off tax on the sale of a residence, levied on twenty houses, as well as a 'tax on sheep', i.e. we have evidence here of permanent settlement as well as of a certain degree of wealth among the Gypsies. There is further evidence of comparatively rich Gypsies, for example, in 1611 the Gypsy Stefan sold his house in Sofia as well as his shop and some fruit trees for 2,400 akche.

Sub-contracting the collection of taxes

With time, the practice of sub-contracting the collection of taxes due from Gypsies (as well as from the entire subject population of the Empire) began to be established in the Ottoman Empire. Interestingly, the accepted practice was that the responsibility for the collection of taxes was down not only to the agent, who had bought the right to collect taxes, but also to the representatives of the Gypsies themselves. According to the sultan's decree of 1638 for the sub-contracting of the collection of the poll-tax from the Gypsies and other nomadic communities, for each fifty Gypsy taxpayers (heads of households) one person, called *cheri-bash*i, was appointed to be in charge. In the case of taxpayers not paying their due, the appointee had to cover the payment but then had the right to recover the sum from the taxpayer's relatives.

Detailed evidence of the tax collecting system and of the beginning of changes in the Gypsies' tax and social status can be found in the decree of Sultan

Ahmet I dating from 1604-5 issued to the magistrates from the regions of Elbasan, Valona*, Delvino, Yannina and of the districts (*ayatollias*) which were fiefs of the Muslim religious authorities of Akarnania*.

According to this decree, the military officer Suleiman (the landlord of this large fief) was given the responsibility for paying over to the sultan's treasury – for the period between 1 March 1604 and 1 March 1605 – the various taxes. The poll-tax, land tax, fees, fines and penalties as well as other charges had to be collected from the settled Gypsies registered as taxpayers, and also from the tent-dwelling Gypsies who were nomads and who were not registered as taxpayers. The local magistrates were obliged to co-operate in the collection of taxes which were set at the amount of 180 *aspri* for Muslims and 250 aspri for Christians, meaning that there had been a change towards the standard taxation of all the Gypsies, and not just those in the tax communities. No one was to put obstacles in the way of this activity and the magistrates were to make sure that 'no other person troubles or oppresses the ethnic group in question'.

The decree paid special attention to the problems of nomadic Gypsies. If they moved away and failed to pay their taxes, the local judicial authorities must find them and make them pay their taxes as well as fine them 300 aspri. Their absence from the district should not be used as an excuse for not paying their taxes. The problems which may arise with the payment of taxes in kind as opposed to money were also dealt with.

[Text] مَقْطُوعَةُ قِبْطِيَان مُسلِم فِى ٦٦. [Below] سِرّى
[Text] Makṭūʿah i Ḳibṭiān i Muslim fī 660. [Below] S[ir]rī.
[Text] Tax of the Moslem Copts in 660, or [1]066. [Below] ? Sirrī.
A.H. 660=A.D. 1261/2. A.H. 1066=A.D. 1655/6.

Ink impression and cast of a blood red Carnelian Seal, bought by J. McG. Dawkins in Constantinople in 1924.
Note: A.H. is Year of the Hegira (Muslim Calendar) and A.D. the Christian Calendar (Anno Domini).

As for the settled Gypsies, the decree dealt with questions relating to taxation and collection of taxes from the Gypsies settled in lands with the status of vakufs or myulks. In addition, it obliged the magistrates not to allow the Gypsies to be 'oppressed and troubled' by the local military administration, indicating that by that time the practice of forcibly attaching Gypsies to land and property had apparently begun:

Some feudal landlords, janissaries, officials and other functionaries hide settled [Gypsies] in their houses, buildings and farms. If this is true, then arrest and expel them. If they do not obey let us know of their names and districts.

The decree made it clear that the Ottoman state had already begun to abolish tax privileges to which certain categories of Gypsies had been entitled:

As for the settled [Gypsies] who say that they are ironmongers, charcoal-burners and fortress guards, and are thus exempt from charges and taxes: if they have not paid their charges and taxes, do not believe them when they say that they are exempt from them, but take from them what they are obliged to give according to the register to the last penny and do not permit them to set up obstacles.

The practice of sub-contracting the collection of taxes from the Gypsies is confirmed in the judicial registers of the Sofia region for 1609 (when the appointed person was Ali Halil Iskender), and for 1610 and 1618. This practice was also described in a sultan's decree of 1684, issued to the magistrates of the regions of Thessaloniki*, Beroya* and Genitsa, which confirmed the right of the magistrate Husain to collect the poll-tax and other taxes from the Gypsies in these regions. The sum of all the taxes came to 650 aspri for each Muslim and 720 aspri for each Christian, the period for their collection being limited to one month (between 9 November and 7 December). It is worth noting the reasoning given for collecting taxes from the Gypsies in this manner, though it should not be taken at face value:

Because this race lives separately and is limited in numbers, but has the utmost respect, let just one person, unobstructed, collect these taxes and charges, destined for the common treasury, consisting of taxes, fines for running away or committing a crime, and above all do not allow any ministers, administrators, civil servants, police officers, courtiers, representatives of religious foundations and of the sultan's property, feudal landlords, or other persons to interfere with the affairs of the Gypsies. Keep the Gypsies well away from wrongdoing against the state, nor do them any injustice or oppress them by demanding more than is laid down in my sultan's decree.

How Gypsies earned their living

Gypsies in the Ottoman Empire worked at a range of occupations. In the tax register of 1522-3 the Gypsies were most often recorded as musicians *(sazende)*. In some cases entire tax communities consisted of musicians – for example, the community of Kara Oglan, the son of Oruch, from the Vranya fortress. In other cases the leader of the tax community was a musician – for example, Boro, the son of Kiriak, from Melnik; Div (or Diyo), the son of Ivrad, from Aitos; the fiddle player Hizir from Eni Shehir and others.

The widespread nature of this occupation among the Gypsies is further confirmed by other historical evidence, including the numerous descriptions of Gypsy musicians by travellers. For example, Quoclet describing Belgrade in 1658 remarked:

Everywhere Gypsies, men and women, play and sing quite pleasantly, using fiddles (*kemanes*), similar to violins, and like the cymbalo and the tambura, which is like the guitar, but with five strings. This entertainment we had throughout our entire journey.

Musicians [Gypsies?]

The musical instruments most commonly encountered in the various sources, are the *zurnas* (a kind of oboe) and the drums – the trio of two zurnas and one drum is to this day very common in the Balkans – but other instruments were also used (most often the tambourine and in more recent times different string instruments). Along with this, there is much evidence about Gypsy musician ensembles (for example, two violins and two tambourines) in combination with dancers (mainly Gypsy women, usually called *chengii*, and sometimes Jewish women), who made merry and entertained Turkish officials (as well as foreign travellers) at inns or at their homes.

One question, however, remains insufficiently explained: the question of the presence of Gypsy blacksmiths in the Ottoman Empire. In many places around the world the Gypsies are known as smiths and this occupation of theirs has a long tradition, a tradition which has been well preserved in the Balkans until today where we find many Gypsy men whose traditional occupation is precisely blacksmithing (and ironmongery in general). Given this, it is really surprising that during certain periods Gypsy blacksmiths and ironmongers were relatively uncommon. For example, in the often quoted tax register of 1522-3 only one person was listed as a blacksmith and only four as various kinds of ironworkers (the names used were *chilingir, timurji, haddad*). Undoubtedly, a large number of the craftsmen included in the Gypsy sanjak were indeed blacksmiths but their number was limited and their work served the army only, not the population of the Empire as a whole. Various hypotheses can be put forward to explain this paradox but none of them sound convincing. This is all the more confusing since there is much earlier evidence from the fifteenth century

Words written down in Romani by Evlia Çelebi in Sheyahat-name, 1668.

about Gypsy blacksmiths and ironworkers and evidence concerning blacksmiths (derived from tax registers or other historical sources) becomes very extensive again from the seventeenth century onwards.

In the 1522-3 tax register, among the recorded occupations of the Gypsies, apart from musicians, there are also tinsmiths, farriers, goldsmiths, sword-makers, stove-makers, shoemakers, slipper-makers, makers of clout-nails, leather workers, tailors, carpet-makers, dyers, ironmongers, halva-makers, cheese-makers, butchers, kebab-makers, gardeners, muleteers, guards, prison guards, manservants, couriers, monkey-breeders, well-diggers and others, including occasionally army officers, janissaries, policemen (*subashis*), doctors, surgeons, monks. It is difficult to be sure to what extent the mention of these occupations presupposes a traditional occupation and to what extent they were newly mastered, although it is evident that a number of cases refer to the traditional professional expertise of certain Gypsy communities.

An important source are the notes of the traveller mentioned above, Evlia Çelebi, who had the opportunity to make use of the list of craftsmen's guilds (*sinifs*) in Istanbul – a list made on the orders of Sultan Murad IV (1623-40). At that time the Gypsies were living in the Balata quarter, having been settled there by Mehmet II at the time of the conquest of the city. The list contained fifty-seven guilds, the Gypsies being mentioned for the first time in the 10th guild, that of the bear-breeders, which consisted of seventy men in total. In the 15th guild were to be found the horse-traders (*jambazes*) consisting of 300 men, and as Evlia Çelebi wrote:

These horse-traders are wealthy traders, each one of them having stables of 40-50 Arab horses; most of them are Gypsies although there are some who belong to other peoples.

The 43rd guild, that of the musicians, consisted of 300 people, also mostly Gypsies. The 45th guild comprised the actors, mime artists and boy dancers. This guild had twelve sub-divisions, the first one of which consisted of 3,000 persons living in the Balata quarter, most of them Gypsies; the second sub-division included 300 boy dancers, also living in Balata, and according to Evlia Çelebi's hints, involved in lewd practices; in the other ten sub-divisions of this guild there were some Gypsies, but not many – Greeks, Armenians and Jews being predominant. The Gypsies were mentioned for the last time in the comprehensive list of the guild of the sellers of *boza*, a fermented drink made with millet.

Conflicts with the law

The occupations of the Gypsies included some considered illegal by the Ottoman administration. In many cases, especially when they settled in cities, the Gypsies earned their living mainly by taking up 'dirty' work, various unskilled jobs or begging, but sometimes also work which was in breach of the laws of the

Empire. There were cases in which the Gypsies got into various kinds of conflicts with the local population, cases which were resolved by the Ottoman legal system. A report in the Sofia judicial proceedings from June 1550 reads as follows:

The monk Nikodim summoned before the Muslim Religious Court [Sheriat] a Gypsy of the name of Dervish, son of Abdullah and in his presence made a statement and said:

'The said Dervish sold me a black horse for 158 akche; the horse was said to be healthy and well, [but in reality] his right eye has gone white and he does not see [with it], he has a defect. I want it returned to him.'

After the claim, which was thus stated, the question was put to the said Dervish who retorted:

'The said claimant saw the defect of the horse, of which he speaks, and accepted it with the defect.'

In this situation, Dervish was asked to produce evidence of the truthfulness of his statement. But as he was unable to give evidence, he asked for the said monk to swear that 'he did not accept the said horse with its defect.'

The oath was given, after which [the court judged] that the horse should be returned to the said vendor.

Loose women

It may be worth mentioning another, albeit relatively rare, occupation of the Gypsy women in the Ottoman Empire. In the previously mentioned Law concerning the Gypsies in the province of Rumelia, it is pointed out that 'the wives of the Gypsies from Istanbul, Edirne, Filibe and Sofia', who are engaged in 'unlawful' occupations must pay 100 akche in total each month. This rather euphemistic expression refers to loose women, as is also evident from the unusually high tax that had to be paid. The classing of a fine as a tax is a formula which is used even today in the Balkans as a means of legalising unlawful activities.

There were even whole tax communities registered for fiscal purposes as gaining their income from this trade. For example the 1522-3 tax register recorded the tax community of Ilias in Istanbul with a special annual tax of 5,000 akche; the community of Mehmet, the son of Karaja, in Edirne with a tax of 3,000 akche; the community of Yaramaz, the son of Todor, in Plovdiv with tax of 1,400 akche. These sums, paid to the Treasury, were very high, especially in comparison with the taxes paid by other social groups.

The existence of groups of loose Gypsy women in the Ottoman Empire is repeatedly confirmed by other historical sources, including the travel memoirs of Europeans, who journeyed throughout the Empire for various reasons. Here is an example from the writings of Captain Shad from 1740-1:

... In Hasalar* [in Razgrad district] we met the first loose women in the Ottoman Empire. They were two frivolous women of the tribe of the wretched nation that in France they usually call 'Egyptiens'.

They were waiting for us ... most beautifully dressed and darker than any Muslim women that live in these parts. They had their heads covered in silk kerchiefs ... their entire clothing was also of silk.

European travellers

The observations of European travellers on the Gypsies of the Ottoman Empire are a valuable source for historians. Naturally, such observations, made by outsiders, were not always precise and consistent with the real state of affairs, but in spite of this they reveal interesting sides to the lives of the Gypsies, which the local sources did not always record but which foreigners noticed. The Englishman Henry Blount writing in the first half of the seventeenth century made the following observations:

I am not one of those who consider them to be of a wicked nature, to be distinguished from others by their filth and laziness, to be the scum of society, and not the result of consecutive generations. Because they wallow in filth and are exposed to the sun, they are more swarthy than the rest. They are to be found in every Turkish city, but they do not steal like our Gypsies, because they are afraid of the cruel punishments. They prophesy your future in the same deceptive way as our Gypsies do, and are, too, satisfied with very little. They use them mostly for dirty work, as street sweepers, blacksmiths, shoemakers, tinsmiths, and the like... Few of them are being circumcised, no one baptises them. They happily clothe themselves in rags, but do not wander, live in shacks and small houses in the outskirts, surrounded by contempt.

Another Englishman, Edward Browne, who travelled throughout the Ottoman Empire at the same time, wrote:

Strong and brave, some of them were bandits. There are many of them in Hungary, Serbia, Bulgaria, Macedonia, and I also saw many in Larisa and other parts of Thessaly. They are more common in the cities, where they make their living with dirty work and trade with craftwork. Many among them dye their hands and feet with red henna and consider that in this way these parts of the body suffer less from the frost. Some Gypsies also dye the ends of their hair. Although they have spread far it is thought that they originate from Wallachia and its neighbouring regions, and it is also considered that in their majority they are Turkish spies.

Civic status of the Gypsies

Very often the question has been posed as to what the general civic status of the Gypsies in the Ottoman Empire was but this question can not be answered simply. The problem is complex because in reality the Gypsies occupied a peculiar place in the overall social and administrative structure of the Empire. The population, as mentioned previously, was divided into two main categories (the 'true believers' and the rayah) but the Gypsies were placed in neither of these two categories. The Gypsies were differentiated through their ethnicity, a rare case in the laws of the Ottoman Empire, although to some extent the approach to the Jews was similar. This treatment was probably the result of their religious practices. As Evlia Çelebi put it 'they celebrate Easter with the Christians, with the Muslims Kurban-bairam, and with the Jews – Shuma-bairam [Passover]'. There was not a strong differentiation between Muslim and Christian Gypsies, either for the purpose of taxation or their overall social status. On the whole, they were closer to the local subject population, with some small privileges for the Muslim Gypsies, and considerably larger benefits for those in the service of the army. However, it is more likely that this attitude towards the Gypsies was rooted in the general feeling towards them under the Ottoman Empire. Many sources reveal the evident contempt felt towards them by the rest of the population – Ottoman and local population alike – who considered them to be a lesser category of people who did not merit any attention, a longstanding social stereotype, which has survived in the Balkans to this day.

In spite of these persistent social attitudes, and perhaps thanks to them, the Gypsies had the opportunity under the Ottoman Empire to preserve many of their ethnic cultural characteristics, for example, their nomadic way of life as well as certain traditional crafts, and ultimately to remain as a closed ethnic community. On the whole, however, the civil status of the Gypsies in the Ottoman Empire was much more favourable than it was for their cousins in western Europe where, during the same historical period (the Middle Ages), the Gypsies were subjected to very cruel, mass persecutions. Perhaps this explains why at the present time the number of Gypsies in the Balkans is much higher than in western Europe.

Official legislation and everyday reality

The problems faced by the subject peoples in the Ottoman Empire seem to have frequently arisen from the way the laws were applied rather than from the legislation itself, a situation which has hardly changed in the Balkans. This analysis is equally valid for the Gypsies and there is much historical evidence to support it. In Bosnia in 1693 the Gypsy Selim, the son of Osman, a baker, turned to the court in Sarajevo with the request to be exempt from the payment of the poll-tax 'as an infidel'. In the request he stated:

... I am the son of a Muslim and I am a Muslim. I live in the Muslim quarter and along with my co-residents pay the tithe when I can manage it. Moreover, along with the Muslims I pray five times a day and send my children to the religious school to learn the Koran along with the rest of the children. I work on my baking orders, and my lawful wife avoids strangers ...

Musician [very likely a Gypsy]

With his request he enclosed his wedding certificate and a circular letter from the Sultan, dealing with the payment of taxes by Muslims. According to the final decision of the court the claimant was exempt from the payment of poll-tax although it is clear that in dozens of other cases the Gypsies did not have the opportunity to turn to the official courts.

In the official documentation from the time of the Ottoman Empire it is not specifically indicated that the Gypsies had to pay the so-called 'blood tax' (*devshirme*) – the taking of young boys from their families to be brought up as future janissaries to serve in elite army units, subjected directly to the sultan. In spite of this, historical evidence suggests that in some cases the subject Balkan peoples used various methods in order to offer Gypsy boys to the Ottoman authorities instead of their own children. In view of this, a number of the sultan's regulations point out that those who attempt to hide their children and substitute Gypsy children for them, will be punished with death.

This has in recent years given rise to the Gypsy legend that:

In the past the Turks used to take the blood tax from each family, marking with a red sign the doors of the houses from where they had already taken a child. In one Gypsy house there was just one child and in order to save it the family followed the advice of Bango Vasii (Lame Basil). They slaughtered a cockerel and spread its blood on the door. The Turks saw the sign and passed on. Since then St Basil's Day (Vasilyovden) is celebrated by killing a cockerel while the children are marked with a spot of blood on their foreheads.

Although legally the Gypsies in the Ottoman Empire were not slaves there seem to have been a number of cases when Gypsies were sold into slavery. In 1533 Hans Dernschwamm recounted that he had seen a group of Gypsies in chains in the slave market, brought there because they had not paid the poll-tax. Similar evidence is also found in reports by other European travellers and in official documents. For example, an official order of 1560 to the local rulers in the Danube region instructed them to observe strictly the rule that Gypsies who paid their tax to the princes of Moldavia and Wallachia were not to be sold in the slave markets. Although slavery in the Ottoman Empire was officially only abolished during the time of the political reforms of 1839 (the Tanzimat) it had almost died out by then and was generally quite limited in scale. In addition, the status of slaves in the Ottoman Empire was complex and varied, often differing from commonly accepted notions of the term. For example, according to the law the ministers were 'slaves of the sultan'. Therefore, Gypsy slavery under the Ottoman Empire – outside of Moldavia and Wallachia – was not a factor that determined their basic civil status and their position in the social structure of the Empire.

Gypsy migrations within the Balkans

The position of the Gypsies in the Ottoman Empire must be considered in comparative terms, and an interesting comparison can be made with Moldavia and Wallachia, the vassal states of the Ottoman Empire, from where escaped Gypsy slaves regularly sought asylum within the boundaries of the Empire proper.

For example, in the previously cited register of 1522-3 in the districts of Shumen and Provadia, two companies of Gypsies recently arrived from Wallachia were recorded – Kulagöz's company consisting of three settled Christian families and the nomads under Tatochi, the son of Slav, comprising thirteen Christian families.

This process of internal migration developed on a particularly large scale at the turn of the seventeenth century when large groups of Gypsies took advantage of the wars between Austria and the Ottoman Empire and the temporary Austrian occupation (1690-1718) of parts of north-east Serbia, north-west Bulgaria and east Banat to penetrate into the heart of the Ottoman Empire and settle down there. Some historians have named this 'the second Gypsy migration into the Balkans'. These Gypsies belonged to a community speaking what linguists call the 'old *vlah*' dialects (*Gurbet, Vlahorya* and other groups) who quickly settled throughout the Balkan peninsula stretching east as far as Asia Minor

The decline and twilight of the Ottoman Empire

After reaching the peak of its power, the Ottoman Empire entered a period of stagnation until at the beginning of the eighteenth century there began the gradual decline of the Empire, a decline which was long drawn out and full of problems.

The crisis in the Empire and its prolonged agony

From 1800 onwards the Empire was in permanent crisis. This affected the social and economic conditions as well as the complex administrative system and was accompanied by a long sequence of unsuccessful wars – mainly with Austria and later with Russia – and the loss of a great amount of territory.

The Ottoman Empire lost two consecutive wars against Russia in the second half of the eighteenth century and had to give up its territory on the northern shore of the Black Sea, the vassal Tatar Crimean Khanat. Sultan Selim III attempted to reform the structures of the government, its administration and economy but this only served to deepen the crisis and led to a prolonged period of internal unrest. Regional and local rulers, now semi-independent, went to war with each other as well as fighting against the central power. The Balkan peninsula was for decades overrun by the armed bands known as *kurjalis and daalis*, mostly former soldiers of the Ottoman army, who indulged in mass plunder of the common people. The rebel (*haidutin*) movement recruited large numbers of the local population to resist these armed bands and the Ottoman administration. Balkan historians have often described these armed rebel detachments as the precursors of the national liberation movement although in reality their activities were often very similar to those of their enemies.

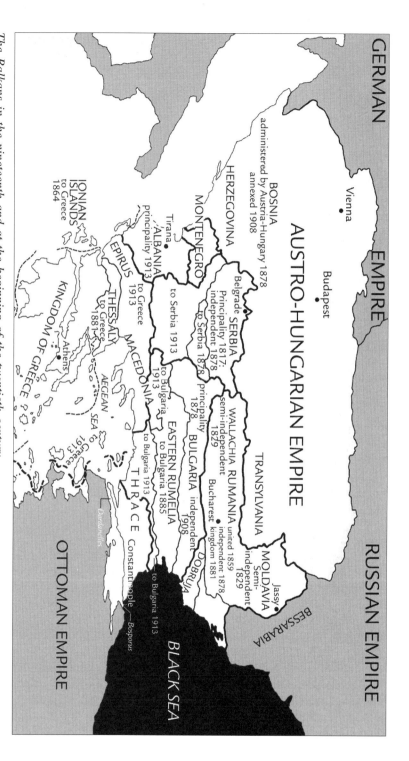

The Balkans in the nineteenth and at the beginning of the twentieth century.

The crisis in the Empire gave a strong impetus to the national liberation struggle of the subject Balkan peoples. After lengthy uprisings and two Russo-Turkish wars (1806-12 and 1821-9) independent states emerged in the Balkans in territories which had previously been part of the Ottoman Empire. Serbia emerged in 1812 following the Bucharest Peace Treaty and Greece regained its sovereignty in 1829 after the Edirne Peace Treaty while the vassal principalities of Montenegro, Moldavia and Wallachia gradually gained full independence, the last two forming Romania.

The attempts at a general reform of the Ottoman Empire in the nineteenth century, the so-called Era of Reforms (*Tanzimat*), linked mainly with the name of Sultan Mahmud II (1808-39), ultimately turned out to be unsuccessful. He set about the removal of the old military-based economic system, the elimination of the janissaries and introduced a regular army, accompanied by land reform and the reorganisation of the entire administrative tax system. The signing in 1839 of the agreement known as the *Gül-hane Hatiserif* guaranteed the absolute equality of civil rights for all subjects of the Empire. All this led to no practical results but merely deepened the crisis of the Empire. Turkey's victory – with the help of Great Britain and France – over Russia during the Crimean War (1853-6), turned out to be a Pyrrhic victory. West European goods and capital poured into the Empire and huge foreign debts increased the economic crisis until the Ottoman Empire became insolvent in 1875 and could not repay its west European creditors. The struggle of the Balkan peoples for national liberation grew fiercer and, following a series of uprisings and the Russo-Turkish War of 1877-8, an independent Bulgarian state emerged. It was initially divided into the principality of Bulgaria and the province of East Rumelia, which remained subject to the Ottoman Empire until 1885 when the two parts were united. At the same time the principalities of Moldavia and Wallachia, together with the Austro-Hungarian Empire, Greece, Montenegro and Serbia, gained large areas of territory from the Ottomans.

The death throes of the Ottoman Empire continued. The Young Turk revolution of 1908 attempted to revive the Empire and to preserve its might but also turned out to be futile. The Ottoman Empire suffered its final defeat during the Balkan Wars of 1912-3, as a result of which Greece, Bulgaria, Serbia and Montenegro divided among themselves almost the entire Balkan territory of the Empire, with the exception of the capital in Istanbul and eastern Thrace.

Historical sources about the Gypsies

As a result of these events the power of the state and the maintenance of state registers (tax, judicial, etc.) gradually declined and documentation of the Gypsies in the Empire became more fragmentary and uncertain. Fortunately, at the same time, there was an increase in eye witness accounts by foreign authors, travelling for various reasons throughout the Ottoman Empire and scholarly research on the Gypsies also began. These sources must always be

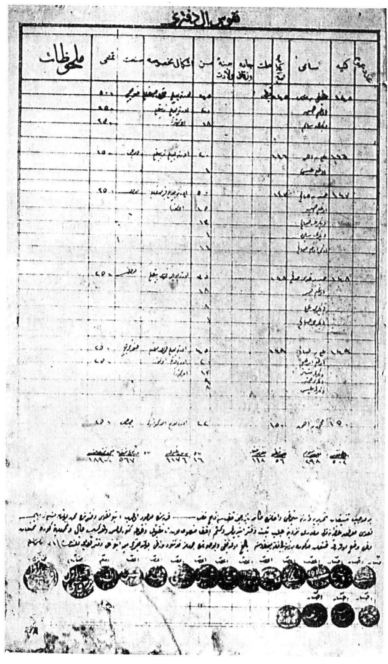

List taken from the tax register of the kaaza of Dobrich (1874). It is noted that the Gypsies who were heads of households in the village of Kadi (today known as Vedrina) included four employed in farming, seven as blacksmiths and ironmongers, eleven as tinsmiths, one as a cowherd and one as a mattock maker.

considered critically but often reveal interesting aspects of the life of the Gypsies in the Ottoman Empire.

The evidence of Johan Kempelen

An interesting piece of evidence, shedding light on the life of the Gypsies and attitudes towards them, is a description of the Gypsies in the Nish area from the travel journals of the Austrian Johan Kempelen, dating from 1740:

... There are about 2,000 Gypsy families living in houses made of woven rods. They have inhabited these lands for a long time, therefore wandering is not so typical of their lives, as it is of the lives of our Egyptians. The women take care of the family and the housework, while the men give themselves up to various ignoble activities, but many of them to crafts. They are put off by agricultural work. Their religion is either Mohammedan or Christian, but mostly none.

... If one of them decides to go to confession, they do not observe any ceremonies, do not stick to any instructions. They have just one wife each, whom they marry after the verbal permission of the magistrate. The poll-tax by the name of *harach*, which the Turks collect from them, is very high.

... Actually, there are no noblemen among them, no chieftain, no discipline or any law. Despised and hated by all, they are the usual suspects after every theft or robbery.

The clothing of the men resembles that of the Bulgarians. The women wear around their necks a necklace with pendants which reaches from one ear to the other and is decorated with various coins. They also wear leather shoes, an overcoat called *anteria*, as well as a leather caftan after the Greek model. Their breasts are entirely naked, they put up their hair in a bun with a little band to which they add an old kerchief.

... For the earliest origin of this clan we can go as far back as the time of Nikephoros around 811 ... [this is followed by a description of the events already mentioned surrounding the earliest settlements of the so-called Atsingani in Thrace] ... From there, it seems, the name of the Gypsies (Zigeuner) was somehow derived. It seems that a large number of migrant or expelled Egyptians got mingled with them. As a result of this it can be said that the names Gypsies (Zigeuner) and Egyptians are synonymously used for them.

... They are proud of this [Egyptian] heritage. However, nothing in their customs and language stands out as Egyptian, or Chaldaean, except for some superstitious prophesies.

Their spoken language is very peculiar, while their pronunciation and their dialects are influenced by Arabic.

Demographic data

Demographic data concerning the Gypsies in the Ottoman Empire becomes quite sketchy in the eighteenth and the nineteenth centuries. The collapse of the old administrative system resulted in the absence of precise tax registers for the population of the Empire. The last comprehensive evidence dates from 1695 in Anatolia and Rumelia when 45,000 Gypsies were registered, with only the men paying tax being counted. Of these 10,000 were Muslims paying 5 groats (gros) poll-tax per person, while the rest were Christians paying 6 groats.

In 1866 the Finance Ministry's official statistics recorded that the total population of the Empire was 42 million people, of whom 18 million lived in Europe (including the vassal states of Montenegro, Serbia, Moldavia and Wallachia). One category of these consisted of 1,300,000 Tartars, Cherkessians, Tsintsars, Armenians, Jews and Gypsies.

Contemporary authors adopted different ways of calculating the number of Gypsies in the Ottoman Empire and this resulted in their totals varying widely. Published estimates for the number of Gypsies in the European part of Turkey in the second half of the nineteenth century varied from 50,000 to as high as 620,000. According to Ubicini there were 214,000 in 1853-4. The Gypsies in Asia Minor were hardly ever mentioned while data for Asia and Africa is completely lacking. There is, however, no reason to doubt the words of Ami Boué when he wrote in the nineteenth century that 'no country in Europe had more Tsingari or Gypsies' than the Ottoman Empire.

More precise data is available for certain regional, village or administrative units. For example, in 1876 it was recorded that in the Plovdiv region the total taxed population was 13,892 (adult men only), of whom the Muslim Gypsies numbered 12,471 and the Christian Gypsies 1,421. Broken down by district the Gypsy population was as follows: Plovdiv – 5,474 Muslims and 495 Christians; Tatar-Pazarjik* – 2,120 Muslims, 495 Christians; Haskovo – 1,548 Muslims, 145 Christians; Stara Zagora – 989 Muslims, 70 Christians; Kazanluk – 1,384 Muslims, 24 Christians; Chirpan – 420 Muslims, 88 Christians; Ahi-Çelebi* – 377 Muslims; Sultan-Eri* – 159 Muslims.

There are also some useful figures to be found in *Donau-Bulgarien und der Balkan*, by the Austrian geographer Felix Kanitz, who travelled throughout the Bulgarian lands during the 1860s and 1870s. According to him, in Kazanluk there were 50 Gypsy houses, in Lovech – 150 houses of 'Turkish' Gypsies and 300 of Christians, in Svishtov – 160 Gypsy houses, in Vidin – 100 Gypsy houses, in Ruse – 500 Gypsies, in Silistra – 58 Gypsy families, in Dobrich – 30 Gypsy houses, in Karnobat – 40 Gypsy houses, in Kalofer – 40 Gypsy families, in Orhanie* – 20 Gypsy houses, in Sofia – 900 Gypsies, in Vratsa – 20 Gypsy houses, in Berkovitsa –31 Gypsy houses, in Koynare – 60 Gypsy houses.

The most comprehensive and reliable statistics for the demography of the Gypsy population in this period are those given by Konstantin Jirecek in his *History of the Bulgarians*. According to him, in the Danube province there were 7,559 Christian Gypsies and 24,835 Muslims (again, only the adult men were counted), while in the Edirne province there were 4,626 Christians and 22,709 Muslims.

The Gypsy population was not evenly distributed throughout all regions and administrative units. All the writers noted that they were most numerous in the central parts of the Balkan peninsula (in particular Thrace) and in the principalities of Moldavia and Wallachia.

It is clear from the data quoted above and in the previous chapter that there was a tendency for the Gypsies to change their religon. During the fifteenth and the sixteenth centuries Christian Gypsies predominated but by the nineteenth century the balance had radically altered and the Muslims were in the majority. The ratio of Christian to Muslim has been variously calculated as 1:3 or 1:4 but it would be difficult to obtain a precise figure. Gypsies often changed their religion but there was a continuing trend over the centuries to adopt Islam.

The ratio of nomadic to settled Gypsies has also not been resolved and once more the criteria for distinguishing between the two were varied and never clearly stated. This may explain why authors contradict each other – for example, according to the French scholar Ami Boué, the settled Gypsies were more numerous than the nomads, while for Dr Alexander Paspati (a Greek doctor from Istanbul and author of the first book on the Gypsies in the Ottoman Empire) the ratio was exactly the opposite.

The latest period for which we have reasonably reliable data on the Gypsies in the Ottoman Empire is for the region of Macedonia at the beginning of the twentieth century. According to Vasil Kunchov there were 54,557 Gypsies, of whom 35,057 were Muslim and 19,500 were Christian but the area he covered did not coincide with the administrative boundaries at that time. For example, the Ottoman province of Skopje included a large part of Kosovo, but Kosovo was not included by Kunchev in his figures.

The Gypsies and the time of reform

The process of reform (or at least attempts at such) in the Ottoman Empire also affected the Gypsies. While changes were being proposed, there were attempts at regulating the civil status of the Gypsies in order to bring it closer to that of the other subjects of the Empire. As with the desire for general reform of the Ottoman Empire, the acts of both central and local authorities turned out to be of little consequence, the circumstances of the Gypsies in the Empire as a whole remaining unchanged.

The Ottoman authorities increasingly used administrative measures to make the nomadic Gypsies settle permanently but in most cases these efforts turned out to be ineffective. For example, in 1805 the governor of Bosnia ordered the local rulers to make the nomadic Gypsies cease their 'wandering way of life' but, according to the reports of the local rulers, although the Gypsies promised to do this, the situation did not change very much. As a result the Sultan decreed in 1845 that the Gypsies in the lands of Rumelia and Anatolia who permanently 'wandered in order to plunder, steal, and do other evil things' would be permitted to settle down wherever they wished as long as the local authorities were agreeable. Furthermore, they were free to travel around the villages and to busy themselves with their crafts (blacksmithing, tinsmithing, etc.) from spring through to the autumn as long as they did not cause any harm to the local population. The intentions of the well-known reformer Mithad Pasha, a ruler of the Danube province in the 1860s, who attempted to ban the nomadic way of life in 1864, remained no more than words on paper. His proposal was approved by the central authorities but was not carried out in practice.

As a result of the crisis of the Empire during the nineteenth century, certain members of the local population in the Balkans ceased to carry out their specific duties and obligations and the Gypsies began to take over their roles. We find an example of this in a passage from *An attempt at a history of the town of Sliven* by Simeon Tabakov, in which he talks about the *voynuks* – a special category of citizens, who until then had mainly been members of the Bulgarian population and who had a number of special duties, such as acting as armed guards of the mountain passes and taking care of the horses in the sultan's palace:

During the final period of the voynuk system in Bulgaria after the Tanzimat (1839) in the region of Sliven – and especially in Jeravna – the duty of travelling to Istanbul annually in order to graze the sultan's horses and mow the sultan's lawns became the duty solely of the Gypsies. The term cheri-bashi has been preserved from this period, being given to the head or the elder of the Gypsy community, while cheri-bashi in Turkish normally meant the head of an army, or chieftain.

During the decline of the Ottoman Empire, which lasted three centuries, the tax privileges enjoyed by Gypsies who worked for the army or served in its auxiliary troops gradually disappeared. No one even remembered them. This is why, in an official report by the Government dated 21 January 1874, it was stated that Gypsies had never served in the army but in future would be allowed to do so whilst the payment of the special military tax by the Christians and others who were not called up to the army (*bedel-i askeri*) would be abolished. This proposal, like most attempts at reform, remained no more than words on paper and the social status of the Gypsies did not change.

Despite the general prejudice towards Gypsies, the Ottoman administration did employ them, but only in minor posts. The author, Felix Kanitz, clearly exaggerated when he claimed that '99 if not 100 percent of the mayors in the Bulgarian villages were Muslim Gypsies' and anyhow the figure did not refer to the actual village mayors *(kehais)* but to the watchmen *(pudars)* who were appointed by the state to watch over the land and were fed by the villagers –

a common practice in the nineteenth century. The Gypsies (naturally only the Muslims) were sometimes also recruited to the irregular police contingents (known as *zaptias*), while during the uprisings of the local subject population in the Balkans they actively participated in the irregular Turkish armed forces (known as *bashi bozuk*) and took part in the plunder and arson of Christian villages.

Mustafa Shibil

It is impossible to establish with certainty the role of the Gypsies in the events which led to the decline of the Ottoman Empire, the official and popular attitude towards them and how it was reflected in their overall status in society. One can only guess, for example, the public attitude to their participation in the kurjali and daali bands mentioned above. By the same token it is not clear whether the rebel, Manush Voivod, really existed. He is often mentioned in Bulgarian popular songs and is supposed to have lived in the eighteenth century. 'Manush' means 'person' in Romani and it is unlikely that a Bulgarian or a representative of some other ethnic community would have accepted it as a first name.

Unlike the semi-legendary Manush Voivod, there is no doubt about the existence of the Gypsy Mustafa Shibil. He was born in the village of Gradets, in the region of Sliven, and was an outlaw until his death in 1856. In later times Mustafa Shibil was to become the prototype of the main character in the well-known short story *Shibil* by Yordan Yovkov, one of the classic writers of Bulgarian literature, although in the tale Shibil is not portrayed as a Gypsy.

Mustafa Shibil is an example of the ambiguous treatment of the same event by different sources and of the inability of the official documents to reveal the complete historical truth. We quote here some papers of the Ottoman administration relating to the case of Mustafa Shibil. First, a letter from the ruler of the Sliven region:

The present letter from your obedient servant is addressed to his Highness the Minister, Commanding Officer of the Army of Rumelia, the Supreme Representative of the Ottoman Empire.

To His Highness

The person called Shibiloglu Mustafa, a well-known bandit, whose origin is from a group of Gypsies permanently living in the village of Gradets, in the Sliven region, along with some of his fellow bandits, roams the above mentioned region and its neighbouring districts, causes damage and loss to the poor people and the Christians, by daring to take away from them their possessions by force, to kill people and to cause outrage.

So that he would abandon his outrageous conduct, which cannot be granted approval, I – your obedient servant – gave my consent and had my confidence in him, yet he, although presently settled and living permanently in the above mentioned village Gradets, he, it became known, still sometimes secretly demands money and goods from the poor and the Christians who inhabit this area, and has again began to be tempted to violence and oppression, as a result of which an investigation has been ordered.

As I report the above to Your Highness, I inform you that I, your obedient servant, have learnt of the content of the written order concerning the matter, which deserves respect and regard, and shows benevolence, and which orders the undertaking of the removal of the evil that the above mentioned person causes – whatever reason he puts forward – so that the well-being, security, peace of mind and repose of all sections of the population and all citizens are restored.

Because the above mentioned person has for several years carried out all sorts of banditry and evil-doing in these parts, during the discussion of the order about the removal of the harm caused by him, when the question was raised of forgiving his previous evil doings, the Christians from the above mentioned village, who deserve respect and regard, ask and insist that in future this should depend on his word being given and on his behaviour.

On the question of providing peace of mind for the poor, under the conditions described above, thanks to written correspondence with the province authority, it was believed that this could be achieved. However, the above mentioned person cannot exist without banditry which is at the root of his nature and his character.

According to the information which has come to me, and which has also been checked by myself, recently he has again dared to perform secretly somewhat evil deeds.

I hope that with your efforts the memory of the persisting evil and of the harm caused by the above mentioned bandit will disappear and will be removed, and that with this every effort will be offered to secure peace and order for the population so that the Christian subjects can go about their business.

As is known to Your Highness on the question of this and everything else, the issue of an order belongs to the one who has the right to make orders (to You).

Date: 10 March 1853
Your obedient servant: Ruler of the Sliven region. Esseyd Ali Riza.

The Army Council discussed the matter and came to the following decision:

25 March

Respect to be shown and an order to be issued by the Temporary Military Court for the following action to be taken.

According to the meaning of the written warning and to the enquiry about the facts, personally made for the purpose of establishing their validity, it becomes clear that the said bandit is not of a kind who could give guarantees or is prepared to learn, that is to say, to mend his ways. On the contrary, he is audacious and bold and should therefore be punished for his deeds, which cannot be approved of. Because of this, all necessary care should be taken so that he is in due course discovered and found.

A written Minister's order should be issued by the Army Corps Commander to the above named Ruler to quickly despatch the bandit in question hither, putting him into chains so that he can not escape during his transfer and that what should be done, can be done.

As is known to Your Highness, the issuing of an order concerning this matter belongs to the one who has the right to give orders (to You).

Date: 25 March 1853.
Supreme Council of the Rumelia Army.
No. 921.

The story of Mustafa Shibil's fate is given a different slant by the well-known Bulgarian rebel and activist in the Bulgarian national liberation movement, Panayot Hitov, in his autobiography *How I became a rebel*:

Much mischief was caused by Mustafa Shibil – a Turkish Gypsy who was bribing the Turkish ruler of Karnobat with 100-200 Turkish lira to pretend that he was chasing him but could not find him. Over a period of eight to ten years the population from Burgas to Sliven, in Kotel and Elena, were crying out to heaven. On hearing the name 'Shibil' they all trembled. Several times they caught Shibil Mustafa and took him to Edirne but he still escaped so that he could plunder and bring dishonour to people. People were reaping their harvests while he, along with his band, went into the villages. On their return in the evening, he would seize them, rob them in their houses and slaughter them. If a trader should go away on business, his [Shibil's] band would notify him that such and such a person was going on a business trip and would travel on such and such a road. In this way the Gypsy had gathered great wealth. In the end, the Turks forgave him, he came to the village of Gradets and began living like a great man, an *aga* [a respected Muslim] and a hero would live. And he ordered that, where there were goatherds in the nearby villages, each one should send him five or ten goats – as they would to an aga so that he, too, had goats in the woods. And the poor goatherds obeyed; who would dare to not send and not give? If they did not they would be slaughtered on the very next day. On top of this, the Gypsy Mustafa took a Bulgarian woman for a wife from this same village of Gradets which was under the authority of the then mayor Vurban Chorbaji; she was called Jenda. She had a husband but since he was like an old woman and did not have a hero's spirit to kill either his wife or the Gypsy – he gave up his wife Jenda and the Gypsy Mustafa showered her with old Turkish gold coins. And the village of Gradets put up with watching this humiliation caused by some Turkish Gypsy! I cannot say that the Gypsy was not a hero. I saw him once when he was in Sliven, in prison, and could not believe that this man – well-built, fair, tall, broad-shouldered – was a Gypsy. But the Gypsy got carried away and began boasting that he, Mustafa, had given the money to the Sliven sultan for the large headquarters buildings (*konaks*) and that he had given this and that to some official. Afterwards, for this simple reason, the Turks sent a detachment of police from Yambol to lie in ambush on the road from the village of Gradets to the village of Kayabash*, and then send a Turk to go to Gradets to tell Shibil Mustafa that his friends were waiting for him to carry out a big robbery but they were not able to do it without him. And Mustafa armed himself, mounted his horse and left Gradets. Before he had been on the road for half an hour, the rifles of those who had set up the ambush on the road fired. This is how they killed the Gypsy.

"Romanies in Roumelia". Illustrated London News, 1885.

The nomadic Gypsies

During this period large numbers of Gypsies in the Ottoman Empire continued to follow a nomadic way of life. Relatively detailed descriptions of the nomadic Gypsies can be found in the writings of Alexander Paspati:

Although they [the Gypsies] are numerous in all areas of Rumelia, it can be asserted that in [the territory of] Ancient Thrace they are at their most numerous. It is a surprise when, during the hot season of the year, their black tents suddenly appear pitched in the vicinity of the big cities as well as near poor villages and small towns. One sees them everywhere, with their tents, and their belongings, and their children, accompanied by donkeys or horses, moving from place to place. Sometimes, there is just one family, sometimes there are more. In the outskirts of larger populated cities, sometimes many large tents can be seen which hold more than one family – the families having stopped here and taken up residence at different points in time, without knowing each other ...

The Gypsies abandon their winter dwellings, called kishla, sometime in the middle of April and then spread out into different regions depending on the time of the year. Some leave the north and travel through the Balkan peninsula as far as Asia Minor while others climb the northern parts of the Balkan mountains and return again in the middle of October. Others, on the other hand, never abandon the region within which they constantly move around, getting to know all the inhabitants of the villages, as well as the needs of craftsmen and villagers ...

They almost always go back to the same winter dwellings, usually camping outside the villages near to a spring; meanwhile their animals graze while secured by their legs to the tents. In Turkish villages, where they are less scorned, their tents can be often seen pitched in the middle of the village ...

The model of seasonal nomadism described above, with permanent winter dwellings, appears to be quite old and also characteristic of the Gypsies in previous centuries. It was typical of the Balkans and continued, with some changes, up to the present time. It is worth quoting the observations of Ami Boué on the way of life of the nomadic Gypsies:

The nomads live in poor tents of grey or black linen cloth impregnated with oil. They pitch these tents at the entrance of the villages or build wooden huts for themselves, covered with straw. Exceptionally, especially in Albania, they can live in carts covered with branches or with linen cloth. Nearby, one can see the oxen or buffalo which pull these carts being grazed, as well as cows, fed by the cart-dwellers.

Most of these nomads ride and when they travel, the company looks very picturesque. Ahead of the file is an armed Gypsy who even has an Albanian rifle, then come the women and children, also riding – even several people on a single horse – then comes the cart and the rest of the men either on foot or on horseback. Instead of going into inns [to sleep], they spend the night at the edge of the wood where they make a bivouac around a big fire ... An anvil and a bellows, some pliers and a hammer, a file and a screw-driver constitute the entire set of craft instruments of the nomadic Gypsy ironmonger.

The Gypsy farmworkers

From the end of the eighteenth century onwards, the sources reveal an increase in the permanent settlement of the Gypsies in villages and their reliance on farm work, a tendency which had first appeared centuries earlier in the Ottoman Empire. The Englishman, William Macmichael, passing through the Bulgarian lands in 1818, mentions 'several small villages' – in the lower Yantra region – 'entirely populated by Gypsies' who have 'settled down and are involved in agriculture' and, although they consider themselves Muslims, they pay the Christian poll-tax.

In the nineteenth century, Ami Boué describes Gypsy villages, such as Hebybje*, near Edirne and Voyniko in the Pind mountain. The existence of villages entirely populated by Gypsies suggests that their inhabitants were agricultural workers. If a village had only a few Gypsy families living in it, the natural supposition would be that they were the craftsmen of the village. However, if the entire village is inhabited by Gypsies, then it is logical to expect that, apart from a few craftsmen, the majority of the inhabitants would be agricultural workers. In the Balkans the word 'villager' (selyanin) is very often equated with 'agricultural worker', since the villagers support themselves almost exclusively by farm work. In addition, it is interesting to note that the name of the latter village mentioned by Ami Boué (Voyniko) may relate to the sometime special population category in the Empire, the so-called voynuks, who have already been mentioned and so it is possible that the Gypsies from this village once enjoyed the status of army reservists.

A further development in the settlement of the Gypsies and the adopting of farming as their regular occupation was the springing up of the farm villages (chiflik köy), dormitory villages in the neighbourhood of newly established farms, from where the Gypsies were recruited as hired workers throughout the year or seasonally. In his detailed description of the Tatar-Pazarjik district in 1870, Stefan Zahariev says that the Gypsies in a number of villages were 'farmworkers and cattle-breeders':

... Yamurlar, 10 houses and 35 Bulgarian inhabitants, with three farms, 10 houses of Gypsy hired farmworkers *(ratai)* and 20 Gypsy inhabitants.
Charganlu – a Turkish village, 35 Turkish houses, 30 Gypsy houses and 100 Gypsies, all farmworkers ...

Vassil Kunchov's descriptions of Macedonia, dating from the end of the nineteenth century, are similar:

... 6. Gulintsi is a farm situated two kilometres south of Vurbeny. There are 30 houses, of which three are Turkish and 27 Gypsy ...
16. Insko has around 15 houses, half Mohammedan Albanians *(arnauts)*, half Gypsy farmworkers ...
19. Novoselsko is a small farm with around 20 Gypsy houses ...

21. Sotir ... There are about 50 houses of which 30 are Turkish and 20 are Gypsy farmworkers ...

The Gypsy musicians

During the decline of the Ottoman Empire, the pre-eminence of Gypsy musicians in society remained almost unchanged. According to Alexander Paspati, who describes the life of Gypsy musicians from the villages in the vicinity of Istanbul, "they go from village to village for feasts and celebrations of Christians and Turks alike, play music and sing"– and Ami Boué notes: "It can be said that as far as [music] is concerned [the Gypsies] have a real monopoly in Turkey."

During the nineteenth century we find for the first time references to public performances of Gypsy music. Although they had no legal obligations towards the Ottoman administration, groups of musicians were invited by the local authorities to play their music on certain occasions. For example, in 1846 at the reception for Sultan Abdul Mejid in Gabrovo two 'Gypsy bands' were invited for the ceremony from the neighbouring towns of Turnovo and Tryavna. The sultan was very pleased with their music and in addition to giving them a generous *bakshish*, rewarded their leader, Baba Tsvyatko with a violin especially sent from Istanbul and decorated with ivory. Gypsy music ensembles, usually comprising the traditional two zurnas and two drums, also played at local feasts related to certain state celebrations (for example, the feast of Testir

Balkan Gypsies, nineteenth century.

which was introduced after the Crimean War in honour of the victory) or official celebrations – for example, the enthronement of a new sultan, the sultan's birthday celebrations or the appointment of a new minister.

During the nineteenth century a new type of urban Gypsy music appeared in Bulgaria, with a modern repertoire which co-existed with the older traditional music. For example, in Koprivshtitsa there were music ensembles comprising two or three violins, clarinet, zurna, lute, tambura and a drum. They travelled during the winter season throughout the European parts of Turkey, extending their repertoire with melodies of various origins and returned to their home town at Easter for the forthcoming months of weddings and merriment.

Closely related to the art of the Gypsy musicians was the development of some specialised forms of musical theatrical performances, for example, the puppet shows. Felix Kanitz gives a detailed description of such a performance in the north of Bulgaria near Svishtov:

Gypsy puppeteers, around 1870.

From the nearby village pleasant sounds and loud laughter could be heard. I looked around to find the reason for this merrymaking and spotted through the fence an amusing scene – a pair of Muslim Gypsies wearing motley costumes were presenting a play with puppets on a string in which 'actors' dressed in French fashion were bowing and moving in a circle to the sounds of a tambourine and a bagpipe. At the same time, the Gypsy was giving his puppets first words of praise, then words of rebuke:

– Hey, hey, not so fast Kara Abdullah, or you will rip off your lovely trousers! – Mehmet, don't gaze at Fatimah in this amorous manner! – And you, lovely Suleima, don't let your dress fly so high, or ... – and in between he was pouring out improper phrases, and on top of all this there were the actions of a monkey sitting on the bagpiper's shoulder and performing various poses.

There are well-known cases where the Gypsies succeeded in preserving through the ages the theatrical traditions of various peoples living in the Empire, a good example being the Eastern shadow theatre of the *Karagöz*, which had once been very popular among the Turkish population, and is preserved today among the Gypsies of northern Greece.

Gypsy crafts

The Gypsies in the Ottoman Empire also earned their living during the eighteenth and nineteenth centuries from a number of other occupations. They were an integral part of the social structure of the Empire and carved out a place in the economy, as Ami Boué states:

And so in Turkey they [the Gypsies] have become truly useful members of society ... They are mainly carters, horse-traders, cart-makers, blacksmiths, coppersmiths, tinsmiths, miners, goldsmiths, musicians, policemen and executioners.

Naturally, this list of occupations did not exhaust the possibilities for earning money. Along with the Gypsies involved in farmwork and those – both settled and nomadic – practising various crafts, mention should be made of the relatively large Gypsy quarters to be found in the cities of the Empire, the inhabitants of which were involved with all kinds of unskilled dirty work. Gypsies undertook some unusual work – for example, in the 1860s in the town of Vidin the number of stray dogs had considerably increased and because of this the town authorities employed the local Gypsies to catch the dogs, paying them 2 piastres for each dog's tail they produced.

Of course, the Gypsies continued to practice their long-established traditional skills, such as trading in animals. Felix Kanitz gives a vivid description of this:

The Gypsies know the art of horse trading very well ... They often dress themselves up in a very special way for the market – with a red sleeveless vest embroidered with gold, and a red belt which pleasantly contrasts with the snow-white shirt which, in turn, contrasts with the brown complexion of the skin and their tar-black hair which often frames their faces beautifully. The motley turban, with loose ends, decorated with palm leaves, coquettishly stands on a lively, expressive head from which gleaming eyes look out for some gullible buyer.

Street entertainer with monkey.

A Gypsy proletariat

Some of the Gypsies in Bulgaria established themselves in completely new crafts, with no precedent among their cousins in other parts of Europe, as in the case of the 'Gypsy proletariat' in the town of Sliven.

In 1836, the Bulgarian Dobry Jeliazkov, known as 'The Factory Man', opened the first modern textile mill in the Ottoman Empire in the town of Sliven, to make cloth for the state – primarily for the Ottoman army. The main work force were Gypsies from the town of Sliven, since at the time the Bulgarians were small craftsmen, traders, or involved in agriculture, and the only uncommitted labourers were the Gypsies (men, women, and even children). Gradually, there was established a working class consisting of Gypsy families engaged in the textile industry which increased considerably after the liberation of Bulgaria (1878) when a number of new factories opened in Sliven and it became an important centre of the textile industry.

The factory of Dobry Jeliazkov in Sliven, around 1870.

The national revival of the Balkan people

Special consideration must be given to the situation of the Gypsies in the new Balkan states which sprang up in the lands of the Empire. For the Balkans, the nineteenth century was the century of nationalism when, after a long sequence of uprisings and wars (primarily between Turkey and Russia), a number of new states appeared (Bulgaria, Greece, Montenegro, Serbia), while the principalities of Moldavia and Wallachia threw off the shackles of the Empire. These states, however, remained in the orbit of the Ottoman Empire to which they remained bound for a long time by vassal status, annual taxation or the presence of Turkish garrisons and retained many vestiges of Ottoman cultural and historical traditions. Even their administrative structure reflected this heritage.

The Gypsies took part in the national liberation struggles of the Balkan peoples. The Gypsy Aliya Plavich and his brother Muyo (who died in 1807) took part in the Serbian uprisings against the Ottoman Empire at the beginning of the nineteenth century, and evidence suggests that other Gypsies were also involved. There were also cases where the Gypsies became the victims of the rebellious local population as on the occasion of the April Uprising of 1876 in Bulgaria when the rebels slaughtered the entire population of the Gypsy quarter (men, women and children) in the town of Koprivshtitsa.

The Gypsy poll-tax in Serbia

A typical example of the strong influence of Ottoman administrative traditions surviving in the new Balkan states was the case of the so-called Gypsy poll-tax in Serbia. After Serbia obtained a measure of self-rule in 1812, the new state, led by Prince Milosh Obrenovich, remained bound to the Ottoman Empire by a number of tax and military obligations. The old tax collecting practices dating back to the time of the Empire also continued, including the special poll-tax for Gypsies (called *arach* in Serbian).

The Serbians retained a poll-tax specially designed for the Gypsies, differentiated according to certain criteria. For those living permanently in one place the tax was 11 groats annually for each person between 15 and 80 years old, while for children it was 4 groats. For those who travelled from one district to another (i.e. those leading a nomadic way of life) it was set in 1818 as 21 groats per person annually. Thus, the idea behind the tax system in Serbia, as it had been in the Ottoman Empire, was to encourage Gypsies through the tax system to settle down. The Gypsies living in Belgrade were exempt from this poll-tax but had to pay various other taxes along with the local population.

The actual figure of the amount of tax to be paid changed – for example, in 1827, this special poll-tax was 8 groats for a child between seven and 15 years old, while persons between 15 and 80 years of age paid 21 groats; several years later, Gypsies between seven and 14 years old were taxed at 8 groats per head, from 14 until they got married 12 groats, while from the wedding until their death – 24 groats annually.

In principle, this special tax for the Gypsies should have led to their being exempt from any other tax obligations towards the state. Thus, despite its discriminatory character, it turned into a peculiar tax privilege since in this way Gypsies theoretically paid less tax than the Serbian population. In practice, this exemption from all other taxes was not always honoured and this led to a number of complaints by Gypsies to Prince Milosh. Much worse were the cases of abuse by the 'Gypsy tax-collectors' (*arachlyas*) – non-Gypsies especially appointed by the prince to collect this tax – who took much larger sums of money from the Gypsies than the fixed amount. This, too, was the subject of many complaints to the prince. Prince Milosh usually paid no attention to these complaints, since he had often appointed his own trusted people to the post of tax-collector as a form of reward. In some cases, however, he showed kindness and freed some Gypsies from these additional tax obligations.

Apart from collecting the taxes, these tax collectors had a number of other functions, mainly administering justice among the Gypsies, imposing punishments, fines and other duties. For example, in the prince's decree of 1819 the collector of the special Gypsy poll-tax, Simeon Logofet, was appointed as the 'supreme ruler of all Gypsies'. He represented the Gypsies in all matters and no one had the right to interfere in his affairs. The tax collectors aroused great fear among the Gypsies. They were well-known figures in Serbian society, the most famous among them being the last one to hold the post – Atanasie Yovanovich (nicknamed Tasa Arachlya). Their assistants, clerks who kept the lists of the Gypsies' tax obligations locally, would have many of the rights and duties of the tax collectors. Gypsy mayors (*knezes*) were appointed from Gypsies in towns and local communities. Their function was similar to that of the earlier Gypsy chief (the cheri-bashi in charge of a tax community) in the Ottoman Empire. They helped with the collection of the poll-tax (or paid it in advance and recovered it later from the Gypsies) and also had some limited administrative power over the Gypsies in their charge. They could, for example, impose fines and make decisions in minor disputes.

The judicial power of the Gypsy tax collector was restricted following the constitution of 1838, as a result of which, in the following year, the Ministry of Internal Affairs decided that court cases involving Gypsies must take place at the Regional Court and that the tax collector must not interfere in such cases.

The Gypsy poll-tax began to disappear. In 1839 the Council of Ministers made a decision, confirmed by the State Council that Gypsies settled in houses would be exempt from the payment of the Gypsy poll-tax and be given the same rights as the rest of the Serbs but when the regional council in Smederevo enquired whether this also referred to the Muslim Gypsies, the Finance Ministry replied that these Gypsies must still pay the Gypsy poll-tax (showing that the policy was not only to encourage settlement but also conversion to Orthodox Christianity).

The process of change in the civil status and tax obligations of the Gypsies did not run smoothly. Although the new Citizenship Law of 1844 gave the Gypsies the same rights as all other Serbian citizens the local authorities often preferred to stick to the old practice (and so did some of the Gypsies as this could mean paying less tax). In 1853 a special decision confirmed that the settled Gypsies would pay their taxes to the local authorities as did other citizens whilst 'the wandering Gypsies' would continue to pay the Gypsy poll-tax. This was now 24 groats for married adults; 12 groats for unmarried adults; 8 groats for children between 8-14 years of age. This had to be paid to the local authorities in a certain specified village, where they had to be registered, and Gypsies whose nomadic way of life took them outside the boundaries of an administrative unit were issued with special passports. In this way the institution of the Gypsy tax collector was done away with, this being confirmed by a special prince's decree of 1854. A number of complaints were directed to the Serbian prince by Gypsies who pleaded that 'their freedom should not be taken away from them' and that the previous system should be retained but these complaints were futile.

The nomadic Gypsies continued to pay the Gypsy poll-tax even after the 1855 monetary reform in Serbia and the new tax legislation of 1864. The Serbian constitution of 1869 affirmed the equality of rights for all Gypsies, but at the same time (along with the Electoral Law) would not allow the nomadic Gypsies to take part in the election of members of parliament because they were not ordinary taxpayers but paid the Gypsy poll-tax. As a result, it was not until the Law of Immediate Taxation (1884) standardised the taxes for all Serbian subjects and the Gypsies were not distinguished as a special category of the population that they finally gained the same civil rights as those of other citizens.

The Gypsies and the religious institutions

At the same time as the transformation in the civil status of the Gypsies in Serbia many of them were changing from Muslim to Christian names accompanied by a change of religion. This was encouraged by the tax policy and was often initiated and carried out by the local authorities. This policy was also applied to the new territories, for example, the regions of Nish and Vrany, which Serbia was given at the Berlin Congress in 1878. A confidential order issued by Melentius, the bishop of Timok, in 1892, obliged the local authorities to 'co-operate' so that all 'Godless' Gypsies would accept Christianity.

On the whole, however, Christian institutions throughout the Balkans were suspicious of the Gypsies and in 1860 a sermon of a Bulgarian bishop said it was a 'great sin to give alms to Gypsies and infidels'.

A similar attitude is revealed in the description of a tragic incident by Alexander Paspati:

In 1866 in a small village near Chorlu by the name of Degirmen, between Constantinople and Adrianople, a group of nomadic Gypsies were camping with their bears. They had Muslim names and were considered to be Muslims from Bohemia. One night, as one of them, by the name of Mustafa, was trying to cross the river with his bear, he sank to his chest in moving sands. His cries for help were heard in the nearby village but since people assumed that the shouts came from robbers, no one took any action and left him to die without help. His companions went to the Greek priest to have him buried, but the priest refused to bury the dead Gypsy because he knew that until the previous day he had been called Mustafa. His companions, however,

Bear trainer, Istanbul postcard, private collection.

pointed out that his name was Theodor. In the end, after the Turks did not discover any traces of circumcision, they gave him back as a Christian [to the villagers] and he was buried according to the ceremony of the Christian church.

Regardless of the teaching of the Church, the attitude of the Christian Balkan peoples towards the Gypsies mainly remained one of ethnic stereotyping, as is shown by a dispatch sent by the village of Ekshi-Su* (in Macedonia) to the newspaper *Novini* (News) published in Istanbul at the end of the nineteenth century:

This village informs us of an interesting incident concerning a Gypsy by the name of Stefan. He was not able to find a Gypsy woman who liked him enough to marry him and so he went to the village of Olishta* with a friend of his; there they hid their Gypsy origin and in this way were able to find a non-Gypsy woman. Stefan wedded her and took his bride to Ekshi-Su*, but in a few days time the father of the bride went there to visit his daughter. Having discovered that his son-in-law was a Gypsy, the father, advised by other people, collected his daughter and took her to the local priest. It was dishonourable and contrary to custom for a non-Gypsy to marry a Gypsy, even though the latter was a Christian. After a few days had elapsed another son-in-law was found and without lawfully ending the first marriage, the woman was wed. The Gypsy was left without a bride. The dispatch justly notes that this was illegal because a second marriage was entered into without the first one being dissolved.

To a large extent, the attitude of the Islamic religious institutions towards the Gypsies was similar to that of the Orthodox church; to this day the Gypsies in the Balkans are usually buried in isolated parts of Muslim graveyards. Also wide spread in the Balkans even today is the old Turkish proverb that in the world there are seventy-two and a half religions, the half being the faith of the Gypsies. The version of this known to Christians also illustrates their doubts as to the faith of the Gypsies and speaks of seventy-seven and a half religions.

Attitudes towards the Gypsies

The position taken by the religious institutions towards the Gypsies was in line with the negative social attitudes of the population as a whole – as much among the Ottoman Turks as among the subjected local population in the Balkans. Ami Boué points out:

The Turks, as well as the Christians, despise them and thus they, neither the former, nor the latter ever want to eat or drink with the Gypsies at the same table ...

Perhaps the most succinct evaluation of the negative stereotype of the Gypsies held by the rest of the population in the Ottoman Empire is given by Konstantin Jirecek:

... despised by the Turks and hated by the Christians ... the surrounding population views the Gypsies as everywhere else – as an impure, intellectually and morally inferior race.

In passing we can mention that, to a large extent, this attitude towards the Gypsies has remained almost unchanged in the Balkans to this day, although nearly everyone is firmly convinced that great tolerance is shown towards other ethnic groups.

The social opinions of the masses often manifested themselves in everyday life, as could be seen in the relationship between the local population of the Empire and the Gypsies, a relationship often leading to situations of conflict which were usually resolved to the detriment of the Gypsies. An event, which took place in the region of Varna in the second half of the nineteenth century, was described in detail by the British consuls Charles Brophy and Stanislas Clair:

The Gypsies make a living largely by supplementing the proceeds from their craftwork with the sale of the produce of their small herds, of butter and milk, in the towns. However, since they do not own the land, they have to buy flour for their needs and corn for their animals from the Christians. For them the villagers put up the price, which becomes much higher for every article sold ... The payment is in money or in labour. When the Gypsies offer their labour, the profit to be made from them can go even higher, as the rates offered for the Gypsies' work can be arbitrarily lowered. In this way the Gypsies are a good source of profit for the villagers.

However, as the spring comes and their herds can graze in the fields, they can sell more butter and milk in Varna, and in this way make more money and be less dependent on the village. The local Bulgarian population then call a meeting of their leaders at which they decide to make them go away, since the Gypsies graze their herds in the meadows without paying for this privilege, at the same time buying very little produce from the village. In this respect it must be added that the Christians themselves do not pay anything for the use of these huge lands with meadows but they make a fuss about the use of the land by the Gypsies.

The pressure that followed was put in a 'delicate' way – one night, without warning, the houses of the Gypsies were set on fire so that the poor Gypsies had to go away. In the winter, however, many of them came back and asked if they could stop in a different place, also near the village. And, since for the inhabitants of this village, Dere-köy, the winter is the most profitable season because of the Gypsies, they granted them permission with pleasure.

The Gypsies complained to the Ottoman authorities but received no response. The official explanation for this was that they had a special order from Istanbul to be careful not to antagonise the Bulgarians.

The beginning of Gypsy emancipation

The nineteenth century saw a new stage in the development of Gypsy self-awareness in the Balkans when the first attempts were made to debate the issue of their social emancipation. In 1866 Petko Rachev Slaveikov, a famous Bulgarian author, published his article 'The Gypsies' in the Istanbul-based newspaper, *Gaida*. The article claimed that the Gypsies came from ancient Egypt and credited them with bringing the achievements of science to ancient Greece. Slaveikov also believed that the Gypsy language had influenced Greek, and explained that the name of Athens was a derivation from 'atsingani'. The scientific background for the article was weak and to a large extent its motivation was to contribute to the social struggle for an independent Bulgarian church, separate from the dominance of the Greek Patriarchy. The newspapers, *Gaida*, and *Makedonia*,were the force behind this movement and Petko Slaveikov was among its leaders.

The article had a considerable influence on the leaders of the Gypsy community. A year later, *Makedonia*, which was edited by Petko Slaveikov, published the following 'Letter to the editor', signed by 'an Egyptian' from the town of Prilep in Macedonia:

Prilep, June 3, 1867

Dear Editor of *Makedonia*,

Everyone knows why the Egyptian people are the most reproached people among all Christians. They do not follow exactly the mysteries of the Orthodox faith, or at least not in the way that the Phanariots would wish them to. [The Phanariots were the followers of the Greek Patriarchy]. And you will see the reason behind this later. Now, if you ask some of the Phanariots who they are and why they came to this position, you will hear the usual response that they are governors of the faith and only they have the right to it, that they are the followers of Christ's Apostles. But if you set out to examine their affairs you will find that they are the very persecutors and destroyers of the faith and its rules, making use of the purity and simplicity of other tribes. They use faith in order to stop progress, to keep it in a harness and slavery. Thus they destroy our Lord's justice that he gave to everyone on earth who has been baptised in his name. 'For all of you who were baptised into Christ have clothed yourselves with Christ' (Galatians, 3:27). They say loudly that all people of the Orthodox faith must be under the spiritual power of the Greeks and no one has the right to have their own spiritual masters. In this so much wrong has been done, and is still being done, today, to the Bulgarians who justly protect their rights. These rights are given to them not only from the Apostles' rules but because of some rights which they have had in the past. But the Greeks persist in their stubbornness and claim, without acknowledging that the times have changed, that being Slavs in spirit they have the right to enlighten the people and rob them openly. How is it possible that they are not ashamed when they say and write such unspeakable things, when even the most simple people know that among the Apostles of Christ (whose task was to enlighten the people in the faith of Christ) there was no Hellene. This clearly shows that it was not up to the Hellenes to enlighten people with the grace of the Holy Ghost. But if only they were, as they will say, pleasing to God, and everybody else was suspicious and unworthy, why is it that the Apostles spoke all languages through the Holy Ghost, but not Hellenic, and preached as Jesus told them: 'Go into all the world and preach the good news to all creation' (Mark, 16:15) but not to the Hellenes. Now that we see that the Greeks were neither chosen by the grace of the Holy Ghost to enlighten people nor were they themselves pleasing to God and loved by him, why, if they are true followers of the rules of Christ, do they say that they have the right to govern all Orthodox people? And why do they keep them as their slaves or even more shamefully, as their property?

But let us now reveal the poor situation of the Greek Church. The Bulgarians and the Egyptians have come to such a pitiable contemptible state that we can never gather courage and educate ourselves, since we have been driven to despair by the rule of the church which has shown us through its councils that we are not pleasing to God. Why do Egyptians resort to two and even three faiths at the same time? It is because, although they are Christian, they are not allowed to participate in the Mysteries, and they are suspected by the rest of the Christians. This is why they resort to another faith, albeit preserving their primary faith. In this way, being dispersed and in despair, the Egyptians cannot have their own society and take care of their own education. You will find the same happening to the Bulgarians. An article in Gaida (number 15, year III) proved that we originate from Egypt. This is evident from our skills but also from our language and the appellation 'Egyptians'. But we have been driven to despair and have turned into what we are now. How is it possible that we are semi-Christian and semi non-Christian in faith? And which rule, according to His Holiness, says that the Egyptians are entirely unpleasing to God? If His Holiness has based his evidence on the fact that the Egyptians once tortured the Israelites who sinned and did not accept the Christian faith, could he not see what the Gospel says – 'Therefore, if anyone is in Christ he is a new creation; the old one has gone, the new has come!' (Corinthians 2, 5:17). Because, if this was not so, then the Judeans and the Apostles should have been under suspicion since they were almost always God's enemies, for which they were punished many times and, besides, they killed the very prophets sent by God and finally crucified His beloved son. But 'Christ Jesus came into the world to save sinners' (1 Timothy, 1:15).

But whichever way it happened, either out of ignorance or from some peculiar whim and hostility that His Holiness felt for the Egyptians, and from his anger to punish them, he forbade the performing of rites for them. And how then could the followers of the Apostles object to this? Yes, they will express regret that they cannot change an iota of the inheritance that we have given them. We would have agreed with this if they were true followers of the Apostles. But not only is this not the duty of the Apostles, it is contrary to what the Apostles should do. In addition, we see that if anything benefits the Greeks, regardless of who invented it and ordained it, they take it, but do not recognise anything that does not benefit them and everything that distinguishes the people within the Christian faith. Although this distinctiveness was made legitimate by Jesus Christ himself and the Apostles who said, 'So there is no difference between Jews and Gentiles, between slaves and free people, between men and women; you are all one in union with Christ Jesus (Galatians 3, 3:28).

Now let us see why the Greeks do not give religious rights to other people and destroy them vigorously. I do not have the ability to investigate why the Greeks treat the Bulgarians in this way, and in any case, I am here concerned with a different topic. I want to demonstrate what is going on with the Egyptians, to whom no one pays attention; I wish to show why their faith has been lost and how this has led to our moral sickness. It has been proved that, 1800 years B.C. the people in Hellas were wild and ferocious, lived in woods, huts and caves, and ate roots and common wild plants and knew nothing.

While the Greeks were oafs and, as we say, were grazing on grass [i.e. they were dumb], the Egyptians had reached a high degree of education, but they caused disturbances in Egypt. A thousand people were displeased with this and moved to Hellas. They brought to Hellas their ancient arts and alphabet. Thanks to the tireless attempts of the Egyptians to educate the wild Hellenes, they were tamed and gradually mixed with their educated visitors. The latter settled in Athens where they made Kekrops their leader and Athens their main town, whereby they took the name Athenians, Atsingani, and reached a more or less perfect degree of education compared to the other peoples living at that time. Thus, enlightenment spread to other peoples, which is why the proud Greeks today say that they have brought enlightenment to the Universe. Being aware that sooner or later the world would find out that the enlightenment had not spread from them, the Greeks decided to attack the faith of the Egyptians who, then hated by everyone, would sink in despair and vanish from the earth. In this the Hellenes have succeeded. Because of the Greeks, St Gregory forbade the Egyptians to officiate. How is it possible then that the Greeks are not ashamed to shout to all people that they were the reason behind the enlightenment of Europe, and for this reason the Europeans should be thankful to the Greeks and help them in case of need? They should blush and keep their mouths shut. If they want to pride themselves in front of Europeans as having brought enlightenment, they should first bow down and prostrate themselves at our feet; they should recognise us as having brought enlightenment to them and do their duty and, thus, show a faithful example for the others.

An Egyptian

This letter is a valuable document which shows the development of social awareness amongst the Gypsies in Bulgaria in the nineteenth century. The author of the letter was well-educated for a man of his time with a good knowledge of Church writings as well as the press. This letter can only be understood properly in the context of the previously mentioned social movement of Bulgarians against the Greek Patriarchy and their aspiration to their own Bulgarian Church. The unknown 'Egyptian' considered this ecclesiastical struggle to be a movement for the protection of every person's right to religious as well as civil equality. The author felt very strongly the attitude of contempt for Gypsies that was prevalent in Christian institutions at the time and he exposed the injustice of this attitude. In order to defend the 'historical right' of the Egyptians to 'have their own society and take care of their education', he resorted to quasi-scientific arguments – in this case the earlier article from the newspaper *Gaida*, the only source accessible to him.

The letter illustrates the beginning of a new stage in the development of self-awareness among some members of the Gypsy community in the Balkans during the nineteenth century. Typical of this new stage is the process of leaving the 'internal' traditional community framework in order to seek an equal place in the new 'external' social and cultural reality, yet still following Gypsy norms and values. The atmosphere in the Balkans at the time predetermined the shape of this new social activity. Like the rest of the Balkan peoples the Gypsies, too, were actively seeking a glorious past as well as the creation of a national historical mythology to support them in their struggle for civil emancipation.

One question remains open: who was the 'Egyptian' author of the letter? Although at first it seems unlikely that he really existed, in the end it turns out to be a distinct possibility. An explanation can be sought in the ethnographic material published by Marko Tsepenkov at the end of the nineteenth century. In a description of the guilds of Prilep he comments on the existence of several Gypsy guilds (farriers, violin makers and porters) which had their own saint's day celebrations (on St. Atanasius' and St. Anthony's day for example):

The reason behind all this is the Gypsy barber called Ilia Naumchev. This Ilia had very good customers visiting him in his shop and gradually came to know the background of his people better. He was not ashamed to call himself an 'Egyptian' because, as he explained, the name came from Egypt. This man hoped very much to be a Gypsy priest. Many years passed and he still wished for this. He worked with the Gypsies telling them not to drink and to behave with dignity. After he gained respect among the Gypsies he convinced the three guilds to celebrate St. Anthony's day. Two or three years ago he succeeded in becoming a priest in Tsarigrad* working for the [Bulgarian] Exarchy.

We can be pretty sure that Ilia Naumchev was the 'Egyptian' who wrote the letter to the Editor of *Makedonia*. Unfortunately, nothing is known of him after he became a priest. But we can be confident that he was among the first leaders of civic Gypsy emancipation, not only in Macedonia and the Balkans, but in the world as well.

The first Romany poet?

The question of whether Gina Ranjičić, described by the Austro-Hungarian scholar Henrich von Wlislocki as the first Gypsy woman poet, really existed has remained unresolved for over a century. Before one can answer this question one has to assess the rich scholarly heritage of Wlislocki himself. During his time he was not respected in academic circles and was despised by his contemporaries because of his links with the Gypsies. He lived and nomadised with Gypsies on several occasions for shorter or longer periods. He has recently been accused by a number of authors, the latest being Joseph Lipa, of falsifying the material which he recorded and published – material which is nowadays hardly ever used by academics.

If we are to believe Wlislocki, he met Gina Ranjičić in Slavonia (then within the Austro-Hungarian Empire) when she was quite old and was incapable of recollecting the exact chronology of her life. She died on 17 May 1891. Gina was introduced to him by the Serbian consul in Sombor (in present day Vojvodina), who, after her death, bought from her relatives three notebooks containing 250 of her poems, written in Romani, the language of the Gypsies. Some of these were later published by Wlislocki.

Without commenting on its truthfulness and authenticity (or the lack of it) we can briefly review Gina Ranjicic's life as it was described by Wlislocki, his account being based on conversations with her and on her poetry, much of which is autobiographical.

It is not clear exactly where and when Gina was born. Her earliest memories date back to the time of the Hungarian revolution in 1848, when she was about ten years of age. At that time she was in Varajdin (in Croatia today). From there, along with her tribesmen from the nomadic Gypsy group 'Nevelya', she escaped to Serbia, 'because the Croats wanted to make the Gypsies fight against the Hungarians.'

At the age of about twelve, in Belgrade, she became separated from the company of Gypsies she was travelling with, while they were being chased by Turkish soldiers for a suspected theft, crossed the Danube and escaped to Hungary. Gina then met a wealthy elderly Armenian tradesman from Constantinople who adopted the girl and took her away with him. In Constantinople he sent her to an Armenian school and for three years even hired a German tutor for her. The Armenian lived with his brother who fell in love with Gina and proposed to her. They began living together, without getting married, and at this point Gina began writing poetry because, as she says in her poems, 'I was very happy with my elderly man.'

The family happiness was destroyed by a young and handsome Albanian called Grigor Korahon who persuaded her to escape with him by telling her falsely that the Sultan had ordered all Armenians in Constantinople to be killed. They went to Adrianople where the Albanian told her that she could not return home because her husband had been robbed and killed by Albanians and she would be arrested as an accomplice.

Grigor and Gina settled down in Adrianople where they lived together for four years. During this time Grigor was an escort for trade caravans, accompanying them to the Hungarian border. On the way the caravans were plundered by Albanian bandits, with whom Grigor was connected, and the booty taken to safety in the Albanian mountains. During most of the trips Grigor was accompanied by Gina, whom he showered with expensive gifts, but they quarrelled over an attempt by her to escape to Constantinople and he injured her badly, as a result of which she had a deep scar on her face for the rest of her life.

Grigor was repentant and to make peace he promised to track down her relatives in Serbia and to bring them to her. He left Gina in Adrianople for three months with a Hungarian man who had moved there after the Hungarian revolution. Gina then fell in love with another man, a Serb, whom she mentions in her poems, but the Serb robbed her and then left her. For weeks Gina wandered around Adrianople starving and in rags, eventually deciding to go and look for her Albanian husband, Grigor, whom she found just a few hours journey outside of the city. He had found her relatives and they had already set up their tents and on her arrival the celebrations began. After several weeks of festivities and quarrels Gina made peace with Grigor, who gave her even more expensive presents. The two of them decided to leave for Albania, while her relatives set off for Serbia. Grigor went ahead of the group to find presents for her relatives who took Gina with them. The company travelled throughout the Balkans for two months and on reaching Albania they found Grigor at the seaside. Grigor then accompanied the relatives to the Serb border where he gave them expensive presents and money, with which they bought 600 pigs and lived happily for a long time. Gina then refused to go with Grigor and the two of them quarrelled again. Eventually Grigor left the group and Gina stayed with her people. At that time she was about twenty-three years of age. She began a nomadic life, meeting 'a gentleman' from Vienna who bought her poems.

During her years travelling she did not write poetry but spent her time hoping that her Albanian love would come back to her. A year later, when all his presents were either sold or eaten, she ran away from her relatives and went to Albania to look for him. She eventually found out that he was on the run, being pursued by the Turkish authorities, probably because of theft, and had joined his relatives in Italy accompanied by a young Albanian woman.

Gina left for Italy by sea. She searched for Grigor in the whole of southern Italy, reached Naples, and from there went to Syracuse in Sicily. There she met a wealthy Jew from Romania called Jacob Hornstein, who was a tradesman, exporting Sicilian wines to Germany, France and England and trading decorative objects imported from Paris to North Africa, where his younger brother had a shop in Morocco.

Gina's new friend was an educated man, with interests in the arts and science. During their six-year stay in Sicily Gina accompanied him on his business trips around the Mediterranean. In North Africa Jacob Hornstein hired a Gypsy boy by the name of Petros Kandalidis to be Gina's manservant. Petros's ancestors had moved to Africa from Greece. Six years later the problems began. Jacob set out on his regular trading trip leaving Gina behind. This was when Gina and Petros, who had grown up in the meantime, began to live together as Gypsies. When Jacob found out he got very angry and sent Petros to his brother's shop in Morocco. Gina ran away from home wishing to commit suicide but when she threw herself into the sea, she was saved by passing sailors. She went back to Jacob but fell very ill and as a result lost her beauty.

Sometime later Gina and Jacob Hornstein went to Cairo on business where Jacob was taken ill and, on the advice of his doctors, went to live in Constantinople. His two sisters arrived from Bucharest to look after him and began feuding with Gina. On 23 March 1866 Jacob Hornstein died and on the same day Gina was taken to prison accused of poisoning him. The post mortem showed that the patient had not been poisoned but Gina remained in prison because Hornstein's relatives, in order to get hold of his inheritance, accused her of theft and fraud. Gina spent three months in prison but was eventually acquitted and released, receiving 10,000 Austrian ducats. Gina deposited this money with an Armenian banker and lived in Constantinople as a rich woman, but a year and a half later she withdrew her money and left for Serbia to look for her relatives. She spent only two days with them, during which time she divided 1,000 ducats among them and, keeping 8,000 for herself, left for Paris. In two years she spent her entire inheritance in Paris, living for a while with a man from Transylvania, amassing debts and eventually being deported by the local authorities to Serbia. The final twenty years of her life were spent with her relatives, leading a nomadic way of life. She died in great poverty in 1891.

Here is one of Gina's poems, translated from Romani. We should not forget, however, that its authenticity remains open to doubt.

The poem by Gina Ranjičić is taken from Wlislocki *Aus dem inneren Leben der Zigeuner,* Berlin 1892, where a German version can be found

A poem by Gina Ranjičić.
The free translation by Donald Kenrick gives the flavour of the original.

Bibactales, streyimases
Taisa isom, taisa;
Nani devla mange dinas
Gule pocipena.

Duripena ne rodavas
Tais jiav coros;
Nani ada me th'arakav,
Isom bibactales.

Kana isom upre bare,
Dala malya kamav;
Kana pashlyovava pro malya,
The sovav pro mara!

Kana cerhen the isomas
Tunyrike raciye,
Upro cunut me the jiav
Kamav me dinilye.

Th'isom nayshukar'der rosa
upre pro Yemese
Ada kamav me dinilye,
Th'isi somnakune.

Bare voyaha tai darha
Lulervav the jias,
Oh kay siges o jivesa
Gelyo the isinas.

Kay the jias, kay na jias!
Me na janav; hoske?
Me na janav, devleya. man!
Ke janel man d'loske.

Kana dures isan mandar,
Mange tut lulervav;
Kiya mange the tu penes
Tut me pergerevav!

Unlucky and unhappy
were all my yesterdays;
For did not God give me
not one sweet gift.

I sought near and far.
I wander blindly;
but find no-one,
how unlucky am I.

When I am on the hills
I want to be in the vale,
When I sleep in a field
I want to be on the sea.

Oh, to be a star
in the dark night.
to ascend to the moon
I am madly in love.

If I were the most beautiful rose
high on Mount Hemus
I am madly in love,
and there is gold everywhere.

With great love and fear
I long for you to come.
Let the days pass quickly
till he comes again

To go, or not to go!
Why am I in doubt?
I know not, Oh God!
Will he understand my folly.

When you are far from me
I long for you.
but when you speak to me.
I push you aside.

The slavery of the Gypsies in Moldavia and Wallachia

As early as the fourteenth and the fifteenth centuries all Gypsies in these two vassal states of the Ottoman Empire had the legal status (confirmed many times) of being slaves of the crown (i.e. the prince), the monasteries or the nobles (boyars). The form this slavery took was not as simple as some authors suggest. The majority of Gypsy slaves were the *vatrashi*, or home slaves who were mostly owned by nobles and monasteries. They were mainly employed in agriculture, practised various crafts, or worked as servants, musicians and in other domestic posts. The second largest category were the *laieshi* (meaning 'wanderers'), the so-called 'slaves of the crown', although sometimes owned by monasteries or nobles. In exchange for an annual payment they were allowed to lead a nomadic way of life and to practice their traditional crafts – for example, as blacksmith, the making and repair of copper utensils, making wooden objects, combs, window-bars and other items, as well as working as hired seasonal workers. A similar status was held by the *aurari* and *rudari* who mined gold in the mountains, as well as other clans involved in different crafts.

In this way a rather contradictory picture of the status of the Gypsy slaves in Moldavia and Wallachia emerges. On the one hand, they were deprived of civil rights and large numbers of them were cruelly exploited, sold as commodities and disciplined with the cruellest of punishments and with mass executions. Impaling on a stake was one method very often encountered. On the other hand, 'slaves' enjoyed various privileges which were unavailable to most classes of the local population, particularly the Romanian villagers. Yet, except for the case of the Gypsy Stefan Razvan, who reigned as Prince of Moldavia for five months in 1595, the Gypsies were, on the whole, considered an inferior social class.

Influenced by European public opinion, the pressure on the principalities of Moldavia and Wallachia to abolish slavery intensified during the first half of the nineteenth century. The legislation of 1816 identified four categories of citizen: noblemen, freemen, slaves and freed men. The latter two categories were mainly Gypsies. This policy of making slaves freed men was adopted by the 1831 Wallachian Constitution (Regulamentul organic) and the Civic Codex of Moldavia of 1833, in which, for the first time, the Gypsies in the principalities were recognised as having the status of individuals, as opposed to being classed as items of property, in accordance with the Roman law on which the legal system of the principalities was originally based. If a slave was killed the perpetrator would no longer go unpunished. Yet, at the same time, the trading of Gypsies was still allowed, including their sale in public markets and the prohibition on marriages between Gypsies and freemen continued to operate – the children of any such marriages had the status of slaves – and other restrictions also applied.

Gypsy blacksmiths in the nineteenth century.

Turkish Gypsies, nineteenth century.

Under the terms of the Paris Peace Treaty which ended the Crimean War the two principalities had to abandon slavery. In Moldavia in 1856 a law was introduced by which the state bought out the slaves from their owners en masse and freed them and a similar law was passed in Wallachia at about the same time. This process took place with difficulty, one of the reasons being the unwillingness of a considerable number of Gypsies to have their status changed from that of slave to free citizen. There are dozens of historical documents confirming this. Many of them were better off paying a fixed annual tax, rather than to be turned into 'normal' citizens with many more tax obligations, no property and limited freedom of movement.

In 1857 in Wallachia 33,267 Gypsy families were bought out and freed, of which 6,241 were slaves of the state, 12,081 monastery slaves and 14,945 belonged to individuals. Precise numbers for Moldavia are lacking, but the number is estimated at around 20,000 families. This means that, if an average family consisted of five members, around 250,000 Gypsies lived in the two principalities at the time. The final abolition of slavery in Moldavia and Wallachia is considered to have taken place in 1864 when the constitution united the two principalities into one country, Romania.

The Gypsy migrations

The Gypsies from Wallachia and Moldova (modern day Romania) with special status were the main force behind the so-called Great Invasion of the Kalderari into western Europe – indeed we should refer to categories, and not groups, since there were many, probably related, Gypsy groups in the category of the *laeshi* while *aurari* and *rudari* were general clan names. They had preserved the earlier traditions of a nomadic way of life. During the long process of abolishing slavery in Moldavia and Wallachia, large numbers travelled to Transylvania and west Banat in the Austro-Hungarian Empire where there were other, large nomadic groups of Gypsies related to them. This concentration of Gypsies became the starting point for further Gypsy migrations, which gradually incorporated large numbers of Gypsies who were already settled in central Europe, constantly moving on and penetrating into new territories. The reason for these mass migrations cannot be sought exclusively in the abolition of slavery in the principalities north of the Danube although this was the catalyst which kick-started a process that had been the result of general social and economic developments during this period. The industrial revolution and the beginning of the modern age in Europe led to the need for major changes in the life of the nomadic Gypsies. They had to find new types of work and escape from the territorial limits of the districts where they traditionally nomadised.

The scale of Gypsy migration increased during the final decades of the nineteenth and the beginning of the twentieth centuries, reaching beyond Europe. It was ultimately to lead to significant changes in the overall distribution

A Gypsy from Yash (Moldavia – today in Romania).

of Gypsy populations around the world. The main driving force behind the Gypsy migrations during this period were the large clans of the Kalderari and the *Lovari*, as well as other related Romani speakers from Moldavia and Wallachia; large scale migrations also occurred in the community of the Rudari (or *Ludari*) – known in central Europe and elsewhere in the world as *Beash* – who spoke Romanian, and often thought of themselves as Romanians rather than Gypsies.

The migrations were mainly from east to west, but the different Gypsy groups took various routes and reached a wide range of European territories. In addition, other smaller Gypsy groups joined in the migrations, increasing the numbers on the move and making the pattern more complicated. For example, in 1897 in the vicinity of Warsaw there appeared a group of Gypsies from Algiers, who had arrived via the Caucasus and Russia; in the same year groups of Gypsies from Baghdad also arrived in the city, leaving a little later for an unknown destination.

From Moldavia and Wallachia the main Gypsy route passed through Transylvania and then split into two. The first route went north-east, crossing Hungary and Poland where they met up with related clans, who had earlier taken the road east and now arrived from Russia. Some remained in Poland and Hungary while others turned west and, via Germany and the Netherlands, reached France, Great Britain and Spain. The second way passed through the Balkans and Italy – where again some of the Gypsies stayed on – and then reached France, Great Britain and Spain. These three countries were common meeting places for Gypsy companies arriving by one or other of the routes. They then headed in groups for Australia, Canada, Latin America, South Africa and the USA. During the course of several decades, working their way through a number of new territories, the Gypsies settled in every continent, using not only their traditional methods of nomadising, but the new means of transport of the modern era – the train and the boat. In this way a new, quite different picture of the Gypsy communities around the world was created; a picture which took on its final shape in the period between the First and the Second World Wars.

The end of the Ottoman Empire

After the Young Turk revolution of 1908 the authority of the sultan's dynasty in the Ottoman Empire was significantly limited and the country took the road of political reform, which, however, led to no early results. The Empire suffered its next catastrophe during the First World War, being on the losing side, and as a result of the Peace Treaty of Sever (1920) had once again to bear considerable territorial losses. After the Greco-Turkish War (1921-2) ended with the Peace Treaty of Lausanne, the new state leader Mustafa Kemal, known as Ataturk, conclusively put an end to the Empire and in its place began to build the new secular state of Turkey. After its prolonged death throes this was actually the formal end of the once great Ottoman Empire.

These final changes were reflected in the fate of the Gypsies still remaining in the boundaries of the Empire and in its once subject Balkan states. After the end of the First World War some of the Gypsies in east Thrace (not only Christians but Muslims as well) moved to neighbouring Bulgaria. The Gypsy migrations were even bigger after the Treaty of Lausanne, according to the clauses of which there had to be an exchange of population between Greece and Turkey. The Turks from the Greek territories had to move to Turkey, while the Greeks from Turkey (mainly from the Asian part) had to move to Greece. Many Gypsies were swept up into this population movement – migrating in both directions and, in this way, entering new territories, although not all Muslim Gypsies left Greece.

As a result of these changes, Gypsies remained permanently within the new boundaries of the one-nation Balkan states. From then on, their historical destiny and their evolution as communities have been interwoven with those of the majority populations of these countries. Each Balkan country set out on its own path, experimenting with the development of various political and economic systems, as well as with different government attitudes towards the

Gypsies. However, the heritage of the Ottoman Empire remains present in various ways – either in the form of established ethnic cultures such that of Islam and the related customs and traditions inherited by large numbers of the Gypsies in the Balkans, or in the form of the influence that Ottoman cultural and historical traditions still have in the life of the individual Balkan states.

Wars, as well as frequent changes of borders have continued to the present day – the most recent example being the disintegration of Yugoslavia and the forming of new states. All this has had an impact on the Gypsies and led to new migrations.

The horror of Kosovo: the legacy of the Ottomans

The status of the Gypsy in the Balkans has always been that of the outsider, as this study has shown. Whether born Muslim or Christian, converted or reconverted they have not been accepted by the priests of either religion, and the Ottoman State reinforced this by giving the Gypsies a special legal and tax status, probably continuing a practice current in Byzantium.

Gypsies were valued for their skills in the army and as musicians but were rarely given office. The texts cited in the preceding pages show that the Gypsies, as everyone else before the days of the welfare state, far from being 'lazy' had to work to earn their living – from the nomads who sold milk to the villagers of the region to the miners in Bosnia and Wallachia. The so-called Gypsy chiefs and tax farmers were rarely from the community. An ominous presage of the future came with the massacre in Koprivshtitsa of Muslim Gypsies, man woman and child, seen as collaborators with the ruling Turks. Gypsies' houses were burnt by locals in Bulgaria to drive them out of the villages in the spring. We have seen similar actions in Romania at the end of the twentieth century in the conflicts over privatised land.

The status of apartness continued into the nineteenth century. During the Second World War the Gypsies were murdered by the German invaders in Serbia and by Croat fascists in Bosnia and Croatia.

When the present conflict broke out in Bosnia the Gypsies were the first to be 'ethnically cleansed' from some areas, as the modern term has it. This was in 1992. After NATO had conquered Kosovo and reinstalled the Albanian refugees, the latter turned on the Gypsies, because a few had collaborated with the Serbian rulers. Thousand of Gypsies have been expelled from Kosovo, once a heartland of Romany culture.

The Ottomans worked on the principle of divide and rule with all their subject peoples and, when the Empire fell, the Treaty of Berlin (1878) drew boundaries which left minorities in each new state. Some say that Tito promised the Romany Gypsies their own state if they fought with his partisans but this promise – if ever made – was never kept. While the Serbs in Kosovo can look to those in Serbia for sustenance and support, and the remaining Jews from Pristina can emigrate to Israel, the displaced Romanies have no country to whom they can turn.

So the legacy of the Ottoman Empire lingers on in the agony of the Gypsies in Yugoslavia today.

Donald Kenrick

Glossary

Foreign terms (mainly Ottoman Turkish) are italicised the first time they occur and usually explained in the text. Below, we list such words if they occur again on a later page, as well as some terms which could not have been translated in the text without disrupting the flow.

Turkish and Bulgarian words have been transliterated in the text according to normal English usage.

Turkish	Transcription
c	j
ç	ch
ğ	y or omitted
ı	i
j	zh
ö	yo
ş	sh
v	v or w
vv	v
yu	ü

ayatollia	land from which the taxes went to a Muslim religious leader (the ayatollah)
akche	a silver coin
arach	(in Serbia), *see* harach
arachlya	tax collector (Serbia)
asper (pl. aspri)	a coin, *see also* akche
bakshish	a tip
baduhava	*see* bedava
bashi bozuk	irregular Turkish units
bedava	penalty
bedel-i askeri	payment for exemption from military service
bedel-i nuzul	stamp duty (UK), once only charge paid on the sale of a residence

93

bey (pl.beyler)	governor of a region (sanjak); chief
beyerbelik	province (in particular Anatolia, Rumelia and – from 1580 – Bosnia). After 1590 they were renamed eyelet.
beylerbey	a rank above the bey, appointed to oversee the beyler in Rumelia
cadi	T. kadı. Local representative of the central government who had judicial and administrative functions. Magistrate.
cadilik	district, under the administration of a cadi
cheri-bashi	T. ceri-başi (i) Tax farmer. A tax-collector responsible for a tax community (jemaat) of Gypsies (ii) A chief. Originally cheri-bashi was a military title meaning a leader of an auxiliary unit, units which later comprised only Gypsies
chiflik	small farm
devshirme	blood tax. Children taken from Christian parents to serve the sultan (the janissaries)
drungarius	a military rank in the Byzantine Empire
gezende	nomads
groat	T. guruş large silver coin
haiduk	bandit
haidutin	rebel, freedom fighter
harach	poll-tax for non-Muslims (see also jizie)
has	a large area of land the taxes from which were granted by the sultan to a prince or governor
ispenche	land tax for Christians
jambaz	horse dealer
janissary	T. yeniceri. Member of elite army units, subjected directly to the sultan, which were later also given certain administrative functions
jebeji	T.cebeci. a representative of the Ottoman administration
jemaat	T. cemaat. Community treated as a unit for tax purposes, usually fifty taxpayers
jemaat-bashi	Gypsy leader of a tax community (in Bosnia)
jinaet	T. cinaet. penalty
jizie	T. cizie. hearth tax to 1691, then a poll-tax for non-Muslims (see also harach)
jyuryum	T. cürüm. fee
jyuryum-i jinaet	fine for an offence
kachkun	a tax
kaftanluk	representative, agent
kaimakam	administrator of a kaza; earlier a court officer
katun	company of Gypsies travelling together
kaaza	district with a cadi as magistrate
kehai	mayor of a village
kemane	fiddle, violin
kethuda	elected mayor of a village or quarter = kehaia

Korban-Bairam	Muslim festival
köy	village
kruvnina	Charge on the first night of marriage
laeshi	Rum. nomads treated generally as slaves of the crown
liva	region = sanjak
mahalla	quarter
miril	leader
mir-liva	major
mirlivash	*see* mir-liva
mirmiran	a high officer
muteferrik	courtier. Nobleman based at the court of the sultan
myulk	T. mülk. Land belonging personally to the sultan
myusyulem	platoon
nahia	district, area. Originally a subdivision of a kaza, later the same as kaza
oda	company of janissaries
ojak	community treated as a unit for supplying men for military duties
porez	tax
pudar	guard
ratai	day labourer
rayah	(i) the subjected non-Muslim population (ii) civilians (whether Muslim or not), as opposed to the military
resmi-i arush	marriage tax
resm-i chift	land tax for Muslims
resm-i flori	household tax
sanjak	(i) region. Division of territory smaller than vilayet (ii) the Gypsy sanjak. In this case 'sanjak' is not used in the usual meaning of a unit of territory but in the sense of a certain group of Gypsies who were involved in a number of auxiliary activities in the service of the army
ser-i jemaat	head of a jemaat or tax community
ser-asker	head of a unit of soldiers
sinif	guild
spahi	serving military officer granted by the sultan the tax income from an area of land (ziamet, timar)
subashi	bailiff responsible for a ziamet of land
terete	a tax
timar	land given by the sultan to members of the military aristocracy – spahis – who would live there and collect the taxes. There were 22,000 timars in Rumelia in 1475
timariot	also timarli; army officer possessing a timar of land
tuganji	representative of the Ottoman administration
vakuf	prebend; land from which the taxes went to Muslim religious institutions
vali	provincial governor, *see also* beylerbey
vatrashi	Rum. Slaves attached to a household

vilayet	province
vizir	minister
vlah	from Wallachia or Romania in general
voynuk	soldier
yamak	auxiliary army unit
yuva	tax
zaim	army officer possessing a ziamet of land
zaptie	platoon
zemi-myulk	*see* myulk
ziamet	land given by the sultan to high ranking members of military aristocracy – spahis. Land larger than a timar.
zurna	shawm or oboe

Notes

Nominally the land in the Ottoman possessions was the property of the Empire and part of it belonged personally to the sultan (the *myulk*) or to the religious institutions (the *vakuf*). The sultan broke down the imperial land into parts (*timar, ziamet*) and divided it amongst the Ottoman military officer class (the *spahis*) who lived on their territories and benefited from the tax revenues and tithes. Larger areas of land (*has*) were given to nobles and other as a reward for special services to the sultan.

The administration of the Empire in the Balkans was divided into two main provinces (*beylerbeylik* or *vilayet*) – Anatolia and Rumelia. These were then subdivided into regions (*sanjak* or *liva*) and districts (*nahia* or *kaza*). These divisions do not relate to feudal ownership of the land but to its government.

For each fifty Gypsy taxpayers (i.e. heads of households) a person, called *cheri-bashi* was appointed to be in charge of tax collection. In the case of taxpayers not paying their due, the appointee had to cover the payment but then had the right to recover the sum from the taxpayer's relatives. The cheri-bashi in this sense was rarely if ever a Gypsy.

The janissaries were Christian children who were taken from their parents as a form of tax (*devshirme*) and brought up as Muslims by the state.

The meaning of several words changed as the Ottoman Empire developed and this glossary does not attempt to cover the evolving structure of the Empire. The book by Inalcik (see bibliography) gives a good description of the system of land tenure.

For the benefit of readers who are acquainted with other literature on the subject, we append a reverse glossary, showing how certain terms have been translated in the text.

auxiliary unit	yamak
captain	spahi
certificate	ferman
company	katun
corporal	mir-liva
decree	ferman

district	kaaza; nahiye
fee	chyurm
feudal landlord	zaim
fief	ziamet; has; ziamet and has
fiefdom	timar
functionary	tuganci
groat	gros
headquarters	konak
magistrate	cadi
mayor	knez
minister	vezir
nobles	boyars
officer	spahi
official	cebeci
penalty	baduhava
poll-tax	haraç (Turkish), arach (Serbian),
prebend	vakuf
province	vilayet, beyerbeylik
quarter	mahalla
region	sancak
representative	kaftanlik
tax community	jemaat
tithe	porez, terete
village mayor	kehai
villein	rayah

Place names and their modern equivalent

In the text   *Modern name*

Adrianopolis	Odrin, T. Edirne
Ahi Celebi	region in Eastern Rhodope
Akarnania	a region situated in southern Albania and north-west Greece
Antioch	Antalia
Beroya	Vereya
Constantinople	Istanbul
Dere-köy	Konstantinovo
Dimotika	Didimotichon
Dyrrachium	Durres
Eksi-Su	Ksinon-Neron (Greece)
Eski Zaara	Stara Zagora
Filibe	Plovdiv
Gyumyurjina	Komotini
Hasalar	Getsovo, a village in the Razgrad district
Hebybje	Lubimets (now Bulgaria)
Kayabash	Skala

Lofcha	Lovech
Modon	Methoni
Nauplia	Nafplion
Orhanie	Botevgrad
Olishta	Melisopotos
Philippopolis	Plovdiv
Plevne	Pleven
Ragusa	Dubrovnik
Sombor	now in Voivodina
Sultan-Eri	region in Eastern Rodope
Tatar Pazarjik	Pazarjik
Thessaloniki	Salonika
Tsarigrad	Istanbul
Tsimpe	Chimpi
Valona	Vlore
Voiniko	now in Greece
Yanboli	Yambol
Yeni Pazar	Novi Pazar

Bibliography

Major reference works

Collection "Izvori za balgarskata istoria" [Sources for Bulgarian History]

Vol. IV   Gandev, H. and Galabov, G. (eds.). Turski izvori za balgarskata istoria. [Turkish Sources for Bulgarian History], Vol. I. Sofia: Bulgarian Academy of Sciences, 1959.

Vol. V   Gandev, H. and Galabov, G. (eds.). Turski izvori za balgarskata istoria. Vol. II. Sofia: Bulgarian Academy of Sciences, 1960.

Vol. X   Tsvetkova, B. and Mutafchieva, V. (eds.). Turski izvori za balgarskata istoria. Vol. I. Sofia: Bulgarian Academy of Sciences, 1964.

Vol. XIII   Todorov, N. and Nedkov, B. (eds.). Turski izvori za balgarskata istoria. Vol. II. Sofia: Bulgarian Academy of Sciences, 1966.

Vol. XVI   Tsvetkova, B. (ed.). Turski izvori za balgarskata istoria. Vol. III. Sofia: Bulgarian Academy of Sciences, 1972.

Vol. XVII   Hristov, H. (ed.). Turski izvori za balgarskata istoria. Vol. IV. Sofia: Bulgarian Academy of Sciences, 1973.

Vol. XX   Tsvetkova, B. (ed.). Turski izvori za balgarskata istoria. Vol. V. Sofia: Bulgarian Academy of Sciences, 1975.

Vol. XXI   Todorov, N. and Kalitsin, M. (ed.). Turski izvori za balgarskata istoria. Vol. VI. Sofia: Bulgarian Academy of Sciences, 1977.

Vol. XXVI   Andreev, S. and Dimitrov, S. (eds.). Turski izvori za balgarskata istoria. Vol. VII. Sofia: Bulgarian Academy of Sciences, 1986.

Collection "Turski dokumenti za istoriata na makedonskiot narod" [Turkish Documents for the History of Macedonian people].

Skopje: Arhiv na Makedonia, Vol. I-VI. 1952-8; Vol. I-V, 1963-88; Vol. I-IV, 1971-8.

Collection "Chuzhdi patepisi za Balkanite" [Foreign Travel books on the Balkans]

Tsvetkova, B. (ed.), *Frenski patepisi za Balkanite. XV-XVIII v.* [French Travel books on the Balkans. 15-18th centuries]. Sofia: Nauka i Izkustvo, 1975.

Ormandzhiyan, A. (ed.), *Armenski patepisi za Balkanite. XIV-XIX v.* [Armenian Travel books on the Balkans. 14-19th centuries], Sofia: Nauka i Izkustvo, 1975.

Miyatev, P. (ed.), *Madzharski patepisi za Balkanite. XVI-XIX v.* [Hungarian Travel books on the Balkans. 16-19th centuries]. Sofia: Nauka i Izkustvo, 1976.

Ionov, M. (ed.), *Nemski i avstriiski patepisi za Balkanite. XV-XVI v.* [German and Austrian Travel books on the Balkans. 15-16th centuries]. Sofia: Nauka i Izkustvo, 1979.

Ionov, M. (ed.), *Nemski i avstriiski patepisi za Balkanite. XVII-sredata na XVIII v.* [German and Austrian Travel books on the Balkans. mid 17-18th centuries]. Sofia: Nauka i Izkustvo, 1979.

Tsvetkova, B. (ed.), *Frenski patepisi za Balkanite. XIX v.* [French Travel books on the Balkans. 19th century]. Sofia: Nauka i Izkustvo, 1981.

Todorova, M. (ed.), *Angliiski patepisi za Balkanite. (kraia na XVI- 30-te godini na XIX v.* [English Travel books on the Balkans. 16-19th centuries]. Sofia: Nauka i Izkustvo, 1987.

Other key sources

Galabov, G. & Duda, H. (ed.), *Die Protkollbücher des Kadiamtes Sofia*, München, 1960.

Ilinskii, G.A. *Gramoti bolgarskih tzarei.* [Charters of Bulgarian Tzars]. Moskva, 1911.

Kozhuharova, M. Russki patepisi za balgarskite zemi (*XVII-XIX v.*). [Russian Travel books on Bulgarian lands. 17–19th centuries]. Sofia: OF, 1986

Mihov, N. *Naselenieto na Turtsia i Balgaria prez 18 i 19 vek. Bibliografski izdirvania, sas statisticheski i etnografski danni* [Population of Turkey and Bulgaria in the18-19th centuries. Bibliographical surveys, with statistical and ethnographical data], Vol. I-V. Sofia, 1915-68.

Sabanovic, H. *Turski izvori za istoriju Beogradu.* [Turkish Sources for the History of Beograd], Vol. I. Beograd: Istorijski Arhiv Beograda, 1964.

Books and articles

Achim, V. *Tiganii in istoria Romaniei*, Bucuresti: Editura Enciclopedica, 1998.

Clair, S.G.B. St. and Brophy, C. A. *A residence in Bulgaria; or notes on the resources and administration of Turkey: the condition and character, manners, customs and language of the Christian and Muslim populations, with reference to the Eastern question.* London, 1869.

Crowe, D. A *History of the Gypsies in Eastern Europe and Russia.* New York: St. Martin's Press, 1995.

Durić, R. *Seoba Roma. Krugovi pakla i venac sreçe.* Beograd: Publicistika, 1983.

Evlia Efendi. *Narrative of travels in Europe, Asia and Africa in the Seventeenth Century.* Translated from the Turkish by Riter Iosef von Hammer, Vol. 1 and 2. London, 1834-50.

Fraser, A. *The Gypsies.* Oxford: Blackwell, 1992.

Friedman V. and Dankoff, R. "The earliest Text in Balkan (Rumelian) Romani: A Passage from Evliya Celebi's seyahat-name." *Journal of the Gypsy Lore Society*, Series 5, Vol. 1, Number 1, 1991, p. 1-21.

Grevemeyer, J.-H. *Geschichte als Utopie. Die Roma Bulgariens*. Berlin: Parabolis, 1998.

Gilsenbach, R. *Weltchronik der Zigeuner. Teil 1: Von den Anfängen bis 1599*. Frankfurt am Main: Peter Lang, 1994.

Gjorgjević, T. R. *Die Zigeuner in Serbien. Ethnologischen Forschungen*. Teil I-II. Budapest, 1903-6.

Gjorgjević, T.R. *Nas narodni zivot*. [Our Folk Life], Vol. I-IV. Belgrade, 1932.

Gökbilgin, M.T. Çingeneler. In: *Islam Enciklopedisi*, Vol. 3. Istanbul, 1945, pp. 420-6.

Hammer, J. von *Geschichte des Osmanischen Reiches*, Vol. I-III. Pest, 1834.

Hancock, I. *The Pariah Syndrome: an account of Gypsy slavery and persecution*. Michigan: Caroma, 1987.

Hasluk, M. "Firman of A.H. 1013-14 (A.D. 1604-05) regarding Gypsies in the Western Balkans." *Journal of the Gypsy Lore Society*, Third Series, 27, No. 1-2, 1948, pp.1-12.

Hitov, P. *Kak stanah haidutin. Familiarni zabeleshki*. [How I become a haidutin. Personal Notes]. Sofia: Darzhavno voenno izdatelsto, 1973 (Second ed.)

Inalćik, H. *An Economic and Social History of the Ottoman Empire, Vol. 1*, 1300-1600. Cambridge: Cambridge University Press, 1997.

Inalćik, H. *The Ottoman Empire. The Classical Age 1300-1600*. London: Phoenix, 1994.

Iorga, N. *Geschichte des osmanischen Reiches, nach den Quelle dargestellt von N. Jorga*, Bd. 1-5. Gotha, 1908-13.

Jirecek, K. *Istoria Bolgar*. [History of the Bulgarians]. Odessa, 1876.

Kanchov, V. *Makedonija. Etnografia i statistika*. [Macedonia. Ethnography and Statistic]. Sofia, 1900

Kanitz, F. *Donau Bulgarien und der Balkan*. Bd I-II. Leipzig, 1882-7.

Karpat, K. H. (ed.) *The Turks of Bulgaria: The History, Culture and Political Fate of a Minority*. Istanbul: The Isis Press, 1990.

Kenrick, D. *Gypsies: From India to the Mediterranean*. Toulouse: Centre de Recherches Tsiganes and CRDP, 1994.

Kenrick, D. and Puxon, G. *The Destiny of Europe's Gypsies*. London: Sussex University Press and Chatto-Heinemann, 1972.

Kogalnitchan, M. de. *Skizze einer Geschichte der Zigeuner ihrer Sitten und ihrer Sprache nebst einem kleinem Wörterbuche dieser Sprache, von Michael von Kogalnitchan. Aus dem französischen übersetzt und mit Anmerkungen und Zusatzen begleitet von Fr. Casca*. Stuttgart, 1840.

Kunt M. and Woodhead C. *Suleyman the Magnificent and his age. The Ottoman Empire in the early modern world*. London and New York: Longman, 1997.

Lejean, G. *Etnografia Evropeiskoj Turtsii*. [Ethnography of the European Turkey]. St. Petersburg, 1868.

Liégeois, J.-P. *Roma, Gypsies, Travellers*. Strasbourg: Council of Europe, 1994.

Marushiakova, E. and Popov, V. (eds.). *Romani*, Vol. I. Sofia: Club '90, 1994.

Marushiakova, E. and Popov, V. *Roma (Gypsies) in Bulgaria*. Frankfurt am Main: Peter Lang, 1997. Über Mundarten und die Wanderungen der Zigeuner Europas. Vols. I-XII. Wien, 1872-80.

Mujić, M. "Polozaj Cigana v Jugoslovenskim zemljama pod Otomanskom vla‚çu." [The conditions of Gypsies in Yugoslavian lands during the Ottoman rule]. *Prilozi za Orijentalnu Filologiju* (Sarajevo) 3-4. 1952-3, pp. 137-93.

Norris, H.T. *Islam in the Balkans. Religion and Society between Europe and the Arab Worlds*. London: Hurst, 1994.

Paspati, Al. *Études sur les Tchingianés ou Bohémiens de l'Empire Ottoman*. Constantinopel, 1870.

Paspati, Al. "Turkish Gypsies." *Journal of the Gypsy Lore Society*. 1 , No 1:3-5.

Petrović, D. "Drustveni polozaj Cigana u nekim jugoslovenskim zemljana u XV-XVI veku." [Social conditions of Gypsies in some areas of Yugoslavia in the 15-16th centuries]. *Jugoslovenski istorijski casopis*. 1-2, 1976, p. 45 ff.

Petrović, D. "Cigani u Srednovekovnom Dubrovniku." [Gypsies in Mediaeval Dubrovnik]. *Zbornik filoloskog fakulteta u Beogradu*, XIII, 1, 1975, pp. 123-45, pp. 146-56.

Poissonier, A. *Les Esclaves Tsiganes dans le Principautés Danubiens*. Paris, 1855.

Popp-Serboianu, C. J. *Les Tsiganes. Histoire – Ethnographie – Linguistique – Grammaire – Dictionnaire*. Paris: Payot, 1930.

Potra, Gh. *Contributioni la istoricul Tiganilor din Romania*. Bucurehti, 1939.

Puxon, G. "Romi vo Makedonija i Vizantija" [Romanies in Macedonia and Byzance]. *Glasnik na institutot za nacionalna istorija*, Skopje 18:2. 1974, pp. 81-95.

Rochow, I. and Matschke, K. "Neues zu den Zigeunern im Byzantinischen Reich um die Wende von 13. zum 14. Jahrhundert." *Jahrbuch der Österreichischen Byzantinistik*, Vol. 41, 1991, pp. 241-54.

Rycaut, P. *The present state of the Ottoman Empire*. Vol. I-III, London, 1670 (Third edn.).

Şerifgil, E. M. "XVI yuzylda Rumeli eyaleti'ndekti Çingeneler", *Turk Dunyasi Arastirmalari Dergisi*, No. 15, 1981, pp.117-44.

Shaw Stanford, J. & Shaw Ezel K. *History of the Ottoman Empire and Modern Turkey*. Cambridge: Cambridge University Press, Vol. 1, 1976; Vol. 2, 1977.

Soulis, G.C. "A Note on the Taxation of the Balkan Gypsies in the seventeenth century." *Journal of the Gypsy Lore Society*, Third Series, 38, No 3-4. 1959, pp. 54-156.

Soulis, G. C. "The Gypsies in the Byzantine Empire and the Balkans in the late Middle Age." *Dumbarton Oaks Papers*, 15. 1961, pp. 143-65.

Speck, P. "Die Vermeintliche Häresie der Athinganoi." *Jahrbuch der Österreichischen Byzantinistik*, Vol. 47, 1997, pp. 37-51.

Stojanovski, A. "Romite na Balkanskiot poloostrov." [Romanies in the Balkan Peninsula]. *Prilozi na Makedonska Akademia na naukite i umetnostite* (Skopje) 7:1. 1974 , pp. 48-75.

Stojanovski, A. "Romite na Balkanskiot poloostrov (vrz osnova na edin izvor of 1523 god)." [Romanies in the Balkan Peninsula (on the basis of a single source from 1523)]. In: Stojanovski, A. *Makedonija vo turskoto srednovekovie (od krajot na XIV – pocetok na XVIII vek)*. Skopje: Kultura, 1989.

Tabakov, S. *Opit za istoria na grad Sliven* [An attempt at a history of the town of Sliven], Vol. I-II, Sofia, 1911.

Todorov, N. B*alkanskiat grad XV-XIX vek. Socialno-ikonomichesko i demografsko razvitie*. [The Balkan town: social, historical and demographic development]. Sofia: Bulgarian Academy of Sciences, 1972.

Ubicini, A. *Etat present de l'Empire Ottoman*. Paris, 1876.

Vukanović, T. *Romi (Tsigani) u Jugoslaviju*. [Roma (Gypsies) in Yugoslavia]. Vranje: Nova Jugoslavia, 1983.

Wlislocki, H. von. *Aus dem inneren Leben der Zigeuner. Ethnologische Mitteilungen*. Berlin: Emil von Felber Verlag, 1892.

Zahariev, S. *Geografski-istoriko-statistichesko opisanie na Tatar-Pazardzhishkata kaaza*. [Geographical, historical, statistical description of the Tatar-Pazardzhishkata kaaza]. Wien, 1870.

Zheliazkova, A. *Razprostranenie na isliama k Zapadnobalgarskite zemi pod osmanska vlast XV-XVIII vek*. [The Spread of Islam in the Western Balkan lands under Ottoman Rule (15-18th centuries)]. Sofia: Bulgarian Academy of Sciences, 1990.

Zirojević, O. "Romi na podrucju danasnie Jugoslavie u vreme turske vladavine." [Romanies in the lands of present day Yugoslavia in the time of Turkish Rule]. *Glasnik Etnografskog muzeja* (Beograd) 45, 1981, pp. 225-45.

Zirojević, O. "Cigani u Srbiji od dolaska Turaka do kraja XVI veka." [Gypsies in Serbia from the arrival of the Turks until the end of the 16th century]. *Jugoslovenski istorijski casopis* (Belgrade) 1-2. 1976, pp. 67-77.

List of illustrations

p. 10   The world map of Edrisi, 1160 A.D. From D. Kenrick, *Gypsies from India to the Mediterranean. The migration of the Gypsies*. Paris/Toulouse: Centre de recherches tsiganes/CRDP Midi-Pyrénées, 1993.

p. 17   Town of Modon with Gypsy settlement, *Peregrinatio in terram santam*, B. von Breydenbach, Mainz, 1486.

p. 21   Ottoman army with army musicians before the gates of Buda and Pest. Woodcut in Lewenklaw's *Neuwe Chronika türkischer Nation*, 1590.

p. 22   Musician. Bibliothèque Nationale de France, Paris. Estampes: Od 26 a in 4°, M 34116.

p. 24   The Balkans around 1360.

p. 33   Decree of Sultan Selim II in 1574. In Vukanovic, *Romi (Cigani) u Jugoslaviji,* Vranje, 1983.

p. 40   Blood Red Carnelian Seal, bought by J.M.G. Dawkins in Constantinople in 1924. JGLS third series volume XIV Part 2.

p. 42   Musicians, Bibliothèque Nationale de France, Estampes, Costumes turcs : Od 6 in 4°, M 34243.

p. 43   Words written down in Romani by Evlia Çelebi in Sheyahat-name.

p. 48   Musician [Very likely a Gypsy]. Bibliothèque Nationale de France, Estampes, Od 27 in 4°, M 34167.

p. 52   The Balkans in the nineteenth and at the beginning of the twentieth century.

p. 54	Tax register from the kaaza of Dobrich from 1874. *Izvori za balgarskata istoria*.
p. 62	Romanies in the Turkish Empire, "Romanies in Roumelia". Picture by R. Caton Woodwill in *Illustrated London News*, 1885.
p. 65	"Balkan Gypsies, 19th Century", in Wedeck, H. E.: *Dictionary of Gypsy Life and Lore*. New York: Philosophical Library, 1973,
p. 66	Gypsy puppeteers, around 1870. Kaniz, Felix: Donau-Bulgarien und der Balkan. *Historisch-geographische Reisestudien aus den Jahren 1860-1879*. Leipzig, 1882. Vol. 2, p. 69.
p. 68	Street entertainer with monkey (Constantinople) in *Musée des costumes* (N° 196), Turquie (41), (dépot 1855), Bibliothèque Nationale de France, Estampes, Ob 30, pet. fol.
p. 69	The factory of Dobry Jeliazkov in Sliven. Kaniz, Felix: Donau-Bulgarien und der Balkan. *Historisch-geographische Reisestudien aus den Jahren 1860-1879*. Leipzig, 1882.
p. 73	Bear trainer, Istanbul. Postcard, private collection.
p. 83	The poem by Gina Ranjičić is taken from Wlislocki, *Vom wandernden Zigeunervolke (Of the wandering Gypsy People)*, 1890, where a German version can be found.
p. 85	Gypsy blacksmiths in the nineteenth century. In Hellwald F. von and L.C. Beck Die heutige Türkei. *Bilder und Schilderungen aus allen Theilen des osmanischen Reihes in Europa*. 2 vol. Leipzig, 1878.
p. 85	"Turkish Gypsies, nineteenth Century", in Wedeck, H. E.: *Dictionary of Gypsy Life and Lore*. New York: Philosophical Library, 1973.
p. 87	A Gypsy from Yash (Moldavia – today in Romania) in *Musée des Costumes* (No. 183), Turquie/Egypte (36), Route de Jassy (dépot 1855). Bibliothèque Nationale de France, Estampes, Ob 30, pet. fol.

The Interface Collection

Interface: a programme

The Gypsy Research Centre at the Université René Descartes, Paris, has been developing cooperation with the European Commission and the Council of Europe since the early 1980s. The Centre's task is to undertake studies and expert work at European level; a significant proportion of its work consists in ensuring the systematic implementation of measures geared towards improving the living conditions of Gypsy communities, especially through the types of action with which it is particularly involved, such as research, training, information, documentation, publication, coordination etc., and in fields which are also areas of research for its own teams: sociology, history, linguistics, social and cultural anthropology...

In order to effectively pursue this work of reflection and of action we have developed a strategy to facilitate the pooling of ideas and initiatives from individuals representing a range of different approaches, to enable all of us to cooperate in an organised, consistent fashion. The working framework we have developed over the years is characterised both by a solidity which lends effective support to activities, and by a flexibility conferring openness and adaptability. This approach, driven by an underlying philosophy outlined in a number of publications, notably the *Interface* newsletter, has become the foundation of our programme of reference.

Interface: a set of teams

A number of international teams play a key role within the programme framework, namely through their work in developing documentation, information, coordination, study and research. With the support of the European Commission, and in connection with the implementation of the Resolution on School Provision for Gypsy and Traveller Children adopted in 1989 by the Ministers of Education of the European Union, working groups on history, language and culture – *the Research Group on European Gypsy History*, *the Research and Action Group on Romani Linguistics,* and *the European Working Group on Gypsy and Traveller Education* – have already been established, as has a working group developing a Gypsy encyclopaedia. Additional support provided by the Council of Europe enables us to extend some of our work to cover the whole of Europe.

Interface: a network

- these Groups, comprising experienced specialists, are tackling a number of tasks: establishing contact networks linking persons involved in research, developing documentary databases relevant to their fields of interest, working as expert groups advising/collaborating with other teams, organising the production and distribution of teaching materials relevant to their fields;

- these productions, prepared by teams representing a number of different states, are the result of truly international collaboration; the composition of these teams means that they are in a position to be well acquainted with the needs and sensitivities of very different places and to have access to national, and local, achievements of quality which it is important to publicise;

- in order to decentralise activities and to allocate them more equitably, a network of publishers in different states has been formed, to ensure both local input and international distribution.

Interface: a Collection

A Collection was seen as the best response to the pressing demand for teaching materials, recognised and approved by the Ministers of Education in the above-mentioned Resolution adopted at European level, and also in the hope of rectifying the overall dearth of quality materials and in so doing to validate and affirm Gypsy history, language and culture.

Published texts carry the *Interface* label of the Gypsy Research Centre.

- they are conceived as being complementary with each other and with action being undertaken at European level, so as to produce a structured information base: such coherence is important for the general reader, and essential in the pedagogical context;

- they are, for the most part, previously unpublished works, which address essential themes which have been insufficiently explored to date, and because they do so in an original fashion;

- their quality is assured by the fact that all are written by, or in close consultation with, experienced specialists;

- although contributions come from specialists, the Collection is not aimed at specialists: it must be accessible/comprehensible to secondary level students, and by teachers of primary level pupils for classroom use. The authors write clear, well-structured texts, with bibliographical references given as an appendix for readers wishing to undertake a more in-depth study;

- although contributions come from specialists, the Collection is not aimed at any particular target group: in an intercultural approach to education, and given the content of each contribution, every student, and every teacher, should have access to Gypsy/Traveller-related information, and may have occasion to use it in the classroom. The texts on offer, the work of expert contributors, may embody new approaches to the topics covered (history, linguistics etc.) and as such be relevant not only to teachers, teacher trainers, pupils, students and researchers, but also social workers, administrators and policy makers;

- contributions may be accompanied by practical teaching aids or other didactic tools; these tools and materials are prepared by teams in the field, experienced teachers and participants in pilot projects. Their output is very illustrative of *Interface* programme dynamics : an association of diverse partners in a context of action-research, producing coordinated, complementary work, with a scope as broad as Europe, yet adapted to the local cultural and linguistic context;

- format is standardised for maximum reader-friendliness and ease of handling;

- the *Interface* collection is international in scope: most titles are published in a number of languages, to render them accessible to the broadest possible public.

A number of topics have been proposed, of which the following are currently being pursued:

- *European Gypsy history*
- *Life stories*
- *Romani linguistics*
- *Rukun*
- *Reference works*

Jean-Pierre Liégeois
Director, Interface Collection

Titles in the Interface Collection: a reminder

The **Interface** Collection is developed by the Gypsy Research Centre at the University René Descartes, Paris, with the support of the European Commission and of the Council of Europe.

1 • Marcel Kurtiàde
- *Śirpustik amare ćhibăqiri* (pupil's book)   CRDP - ISBN: 2-86565-074-X
- Teacher's manual available in: Albanian, English, French, Polish, Romanian, Slovak and Spanish (each with its own ISBN).

2 • Antonio Gómez Alfaro
- *La Gran redada de Gitanos*   PG - ISBN: 84-87347-09-6
- *The Great Gypsy Round-up*   PG - ISBN: 84-87347-12-6
- *La Grande rafle des Gltans*   CRDP - ISBN. 2-86565-083-9
- *La grande retata dei Gitani*   ANICIA/CSZ: 88-900078-2-6
- *Marea prigonire a Rromilor*   EA - ISBN: 973-9216-35-8
- *Die große Razzia gegen die Gitanos*   PA - ISBN: 3-88402-199-0
- *Velk proticikánsk zátah*   VUP - ISBN: 80-7067-917-4

3 • Donald Kenrick
- *Gypsies: from India to the Mediterranean*   CRDP - ISBN: 2-86565-082-0
- *Los Gitanos: de la India al Mediterráneo*   PG - ISBN: 84-87347-13-4
- *Les Tsiganes de l'Inde à la Méditerranée*   CRDP - ISBN: 2-86565-081-2
- *Zingari: dall'India al Mediterraneo*   ANICIA/CSZ: 88-900078-1-8
- *Τσιγγάνοι : από τις Ινδίες σιn Μεσόγειο*   EK - ISBN: 960-03-1834-4
- *Циганите : от Индия до Средиземно море*   LIT - ISBN: 954-8537-56-7
- *Rromii: din India la Mediterana*   EA - ISBN: 973-9216-36-6
- *Sinti und Roma: Von Indien bis zum Mittelmeer*   PA - ISBN: 3-88402-201-6
- *Ciganos: da Índia ao Mediterrâneo*   SE - ISBN: 972-8339-15-1
- *Romengiro Drom: Indijatyr ke Maškiratuno Derjav*   PA - ISBN: 3-88402-241-5

4 • Elisa Mª Lopes da Costa
- *Os Ciganos: Fontes bibliográficas em Portugal*   PG - ISBN: 84-87347-11-8

5 • Marielle Danbakli
- *Textes des institutions internationales concernant les Tsiganes*   CRDP - ISBN: 2-86565-098-7
- *On Gypsies: Texts issued by International Institutions*   CRDP - ISBN: 2-86565-099-5
- *Текстове на международните институции за циганите*   LIT - ISBN: 954-8537-53-2

6 • Bernard Leblon
- *Gitans et flamenco*   CRDP - ISBN: 2-86565-107-X
- *Gypsies and Flamenco*   UHP - ISBN: 0 900 45859-3
- *Gitani e flamenco*   ANICIA/CSZ: 88-900078-8-5
- *Gitanos und Flamenco*   PA - ISBN: 3-88402-198-2

7 • David Mayall
- *English Gypsies and State Policies*   UHP - ISBN: 0 900 458 64 X

8 • D. Kenrick, G. Puxon
- *Gypsies under the Swastika*   UHP - ISBN: 0 900 458 65 8

- *Gitanos bajo la Cruz Gamada* — PG - ISBN: 84-87347-16-9
- *Les Tsiganes sous l'oppression nazie* — CRDP - ISBN: 2-86565-172-X
- *Хитлеризмът и циганите* — LIT - ISBN: 954-8537-57-5
- *Os Ciganos sob o domínio da suástica* — SE - ISBN: 972-8339-16-X
- *Cikáni pod hákovým křížem* — VUP - ISBN: 80-244-0048-0

9 • Giorgio Viaggio
- *Storia degli Zingari in Italia* — ANICIA/CSZ: 88-900078-9-3

10 • D. Kenrick, G. Puxon
- *Bibaxtale Berśa* — PG - ISBN: 84-87347-15-0

11 • Jean-Pierre Liégeois
- *Minorité et scolarité : le parcours tsigane* — CRDP - ISBN: 2-86565-192-4
- *School Provision for Ethnic Minorities: The Gypsy Paradigm* — UHP - ISBN: 0 900 458 88 7
- *Minoría y Escolaridad: el Paradigma Gitano* — PG - ISBN: 84-87347-17-7
- *Die schulische Betreuung ethnischer Minderheiten: Das Beispiel der Sinti und Roma* — PA - ISBN: 3-88402-200-8
- *Minoranza e scuola: il percorso zingaro* — ANICIA - ISBN: 88-900078-

12 • K. Fings, H. Heuß, F. Sparing
- *Von der "Rassenforschung" zu den Lagern Sinti und Roma unter dem Nazi-Regime - 1* — PA - ISBN: 3-88402-188-5
- *De la "science raciale" aux camps Les Tsiganes dans la Seconde Guerre mondiale - 1* — CRDP - ISBN: 2-86565-186-X
- *From "Race Science" to the Camps The Gypsies during the Second World War - 1* — UHP - ISBN: 0 900 458 78 X
- *Dalla "ricerca razziale" ai campi nazisti Gli Zingari nella Seconda Guerra mondiale - 1* — ANICIA/CSZ: 88-900078-3-4
- *De la "ştiinţa" rasială la lagărele de exterminare Rromii în perioada regimului nazist - 1* — EA - ISBN: 973-9216-68-4
- *De la "ciencia de las razas" a los campos de exterminio Sinti y Romá bajo el Régimen Nazi - 1* — PG - ISBN: 84-87347-20-7

13 • Joint authorship
- *In the shadow of the Swastika The Gypsies during the Second World War - 2* — UHP - ISBN: 0 900 458 85 2
- *Sinti und Roma unter dem Nazi-Regime - 2 Die Verfolgung im besetzten Europa* — PA - ISBN: 3-88402-240-7

14 • G. Donzello, B. M. Karpati
- *Un ragazzo zingaro nella mia classe* — ANICIA/CSZ: 88-900078-4-2

15 • A. Gómez Alfaro, E. M. Lopes da Costa, S. Sillers Floate
- *Deportaciones de Gitanos* — PG - ISBN: 84-87347-18-5
- *Ciganos e degredos* — SE - ISBN: 972-8339-24-0

16 • Ilona Lacková
- *A false dawn. My life as a Gypsy woman in Slovakia* — UHP - ISBN: 1-902806-00-X
- *Je suis née sous une bonne étoile… Ma vie de femme tsigane en Slovaquie* — HA - ISBN: 2-7384-8756-4

• *Родена съм под щастлива звезда*
Моят живот на циганка в Словакия   LIT - ISBN : 954-8537-76-1

17 • Жан-Пиер Лиежоа
- *Роми, Цигани, Чергари*   LIT - ISBN : 954-853-63-X

18 • Reimar Gilsenbach
- *Von Tschudemann zu Seemann*
Zwei Prozesse aus der Geschichte deutscher Sinti   PA - ISBN: 3-88402-202-4

19 • Jeremy Sandford
- *Rokkering to the Gorjios*   UHP - ISBN: 1 902806 04 2

20 • Joint authorship
- *Europa se burla del Racismo Antología
internacional de humor antirracista*   PG - ISBN: 84-87347-23-1
- *L'Europe se moque du racisme,
Anthologie internationale d'humour antiraciste*
- *Europa pfeift auf den Rassismus,
Internationale Anthologie des antirassistischen Humors*
- *Europe mocks Racism, International Anthology of Anti-Racist Humour*
- *L'Europa si beffa del Razzismo, Antologia internazionale di umorismo antirazzista*

21 • Joint authorship
- *What is the Romani language?*   UHP - ISBN: 1 902806 06 9

22 • Elena Marushiakova, Vesselin Popov
- *Циганите В Османската империя*   LIT - ISBN: 954-8537-65-6
- *Gypsies in the Ottoman Empire:
a contribution to the history of the Balkans*   UHP-ISBN: 1 902806 02 6

23 • Joint authorship
- *La Chiesa cattolica e gli Zingari*   ANICIA/CSZ: 88-900078-5-0

25 • Joint authorship
- *Ромски кръстопъти*   LIT - ISBN : 954-8537-77-X

The Rukun Series:

- *O Rukun ʒal and-i skòla*
Groupe de recherche et d'action en linguistique romani
Research and Action Group on Romani Linguistics   RB - ISBN: 2-9507850-1-8
- *Kaj si o Rukun amaro ?*   Idem
RB - ISBN: 2-9507850-2-6

I bari lavenqi pustik e Rukunesqiri   Idem
- English: *Spot's Big Book of Words* /
French: *Le grand livre des mots de Spot*   RB - ISBN: 2-9507850-3-4
- Castellano: *El gran libro de las palavras de Rukún*
Português: *O grande livro das palavras de Rukún*   PG - ISBN: 84-87347-22-3

All orders, whether direct or through a bookshop, should be addressed directly to the relevant publisher. Generally speaking, the publishers will be able to offer discounts for bulk purchase by associations, administrative bodies, schools etc. Inter-publisher agreements should make all titles easily obtainable: for example the English version of *From India to the Mediterranean* can be ordered from UHP, customers in Spain should contact their local supplier, PG, for copies of *Śirpustik amare ćhibăqiri*, etc.

Publishers' addresses:

- **ANICIA**
Via San Francesco a Ripa, 62
I - 00153 Roma

- **CRDP** –
Centre Régional de Documentation
Pédagogique Midi-Pyrénées
3 rue Roquelaine
F - 31069 Toulouse Cedex

- **EA** – Editura Alternative
Casa Presei, Corp. A, Et. 6
Piaţa Presei Libere, 1
RO - 71341 Bucureşti 1

- **EK** – Editions Kastaniotis /
ΕΚΔΟΣΕΙΣ ΚΑΣΤΑΝΙΩΤΗ
11, Zalogou
GR - 106 78 Athènes

- **HA** – Editions L'Harmattan
5-7, rue de l'Ecole Polytechnique
F - 75005 Paris
  - *distribution in Belgium*
  - *distribution in Canada*
  - *distribution in Switzerland*

- **LIT** – Maison d'Edition Litavra /
за Литавра
163 A - Rakovski
BG - 1000 Sofia

- **PA** – Edition Parabolis
Schliemannstraße 23
D - 10437 Berlin

- **PG** – Editorial Presencia Gitana
Valderrodrigo, 76 y 78
E - 28039 Madrid

- **SE** – Entreculturas /
Secretariado Coordenador
dos Programas de Educação Multicultural
Trav. das Terras de Sant'Ana, 15 - 1°
PT - 1250 Lisboa

- **UHP** – University of Hertfordshire
Press
College Lane - Hatfield
UK - Hertfordshire AL10 9AB
  - *distribution in Ireland*
  - *distribution in USA*

- **VUP** – Univerzita Palackého v
Olomouci - Vydavatelství
Palacky University Press
Křížkovského 8
CZ - 771 47 Olomouc

- *distribution for some Rukun titles:*
RB – Rromani Baxt
22, rue du Port
F - 63000 Clermont-Ferrand